# The Black Prince

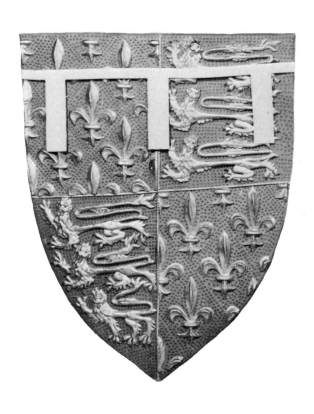

# The
# Black Prince

## Hubert Cole

Book Club Edition

This edition published by
Purnell Book Services Limited
Milton, Nr. Abingdon, Oxon OX14 4HE.
By arrangement with Granada Publishing Limited.

Printed in Great Britain by
Butler & Tanner Ltd, Frome and London

*For Bridget*

# List of Maps

# Introduction

In the history of all nations there are periods when it seems that a particular national group cannot fail in any of its enterprises; it has, as it were, a 'golden touch' in whatever it attempts. The Swedes under Gustavus Adolphus, the French in the hey-day of Louis XIV or Napoleon, Prussia under Bismarck are all cases in point. England, too, had its 'finest hours' long before Winston Churchill applied the phrase to a very bleak hour indeed: there was the first Elizabethan age, or the period of Nelson, Moore and Wellington, when victory followed victory, and prestige abounded.

The first of such periods in English history, often forgotten, is that covered in this book by Hubert Cole. It is the early part of the reign of Edward III, the time when English national identity was forged in battle against the Scots, the French and the Spanish. The middle of the fourteenth century saw a remarkable flowering of chivalry in England, with great names abounding: the Dukes of Lancaster, William de Bohun Earl of Northampton, Sir John Chandos, Sir Robert Knollys – but no name more renowned than that of the king's eldest son, Edward Prince of Wales, the Black Prince.

It was precisely the span of the Black Prince's active life that contained the zenith of English fame, when English men-at-arms and English archers together won themselves the reputation of 'the finest and most daring warriors known to man'. At the age of sixteen, the Black Prince, at the Battle of Crécy, played a great part in laying the foundations of this fame. In 1356 he secured it – and his own – with his victory at Poitiers. He wrote its last chapter in 1367 at Nájera in Castile. Thereafter, with the physical decline of the Black Prince, both his father's renown and England's diminished together. Hubert Cole here tells us the story of greatness tinged with high tragedy.

John Terraine

# Contents

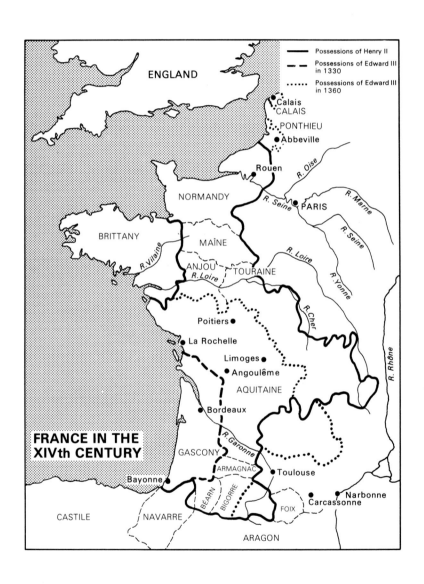

ENGLAND

Calais
CALAIS
PONTHIEU
Abbeville

Rouen

R. Oise

NORMANDY

R. Seine • PARIS

R. Marne

R. Seine

BRITTANY

MAÎNE

R. Vilaine

ANJOU
R. Loire

TOURAINE

R. Loire

R. Yonne

R. Cher

Poitiers ●

La Rochelle ●

Limoges ●
● Angoulême

AQUITAINE

● Bordeaux

R. Rhône

FRANCE IN THE
XIVth CENTURY

GASCONY

R. Garonne

ARMAGNAC

Bayonne ●

● Toulouse

BÉARN

BIGORRE

FOIX

● Narbonne
Carcassonne ●

CASTILE

NAVARRE

ARAGON

——— Possessions of Henry II

– – – Possessions of Edward III
in 1330

········· Possessions of Edward III
in 1360

Chapter One

# ℋeritage

It was 29 September 1376, the feast of St Michael, Prince of Angels, Commander of the Heavenly Hosts. The embalmed body that had lain in state in the Palace of Westminster since June was sealed in a lead coffin and carried to the hearse drawn by twelve black horses. Upon the silken pall that covered the coffin was set the dead man's helm, scarred by the dint of battle and surmounted by his crest: the gilded lion on an ermine-lined cap of maintenance. Above the blankly staring eye-slits the forged iron bar that joined the skull and face piece ended in a fleur-de-lys; the small ventilation holes in the right cheek were patterned like a crown; a chain hung from the metal point of the chin to secure the helm to the breastplate. Beside the helm lay the empty gilded copper gauntlets embossed with lions at the knuckles; the great sword undrawn in its red leather scabbard; the shield and embroidered surcoat, blazing with the blue, red and gold of the lilies of France quartered with the lions of England, cadenced with the white three-pointed label of an eldest son.

The procession moved off along the slow curve of the Thames, through the fields to the City, from the City out across London Bridge to Southwark and so up to Blackheath and the long road to Canterbury. There, as the cortège entered the West Gate, it re-formed: at the head, two destriers, the mighty-muscled war-horses, barded and caparisoned. Behind them, two fully armoured knights, one carrying the prince's shield of war, the royal arms and the motto *Homout*, High Courage, the other with his badge of peace, the silver ostrich plumes and the legend *Ich dene*, I serve. And following them, four of the sable banners that had given him the name by which he was to be

'The gilded copper gauntlets embossed with lions at the knuckles' reconstructed from the Black Prince's original pair.

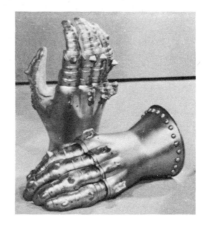

'The helm surmounted by his crest: the gilded lion on an ermine-lined cap of maintenance' (replica).

10

known to history: The Black Prince – 'the chief flower of all chivalry' – Edward of Woodstock, Prince of Wales, Duke of Cornwall, Earl of Chester, one-time Prince of Aquitaine.

'Who departing, all hope of Englishmen departed, for he being present they feared not the incursions of any enemies, nor the forcible meeting in battle.' The citizens of Canterbury stood silent, awed and sorrowful, as the famous warrior son of their warrior king passed on his way to burial in the cathedral.

'The shield and embroidered surcoat, blazing with the blue, red and gold of the lilies of France quartered with the lions of England, cadenced with the white three-pointed label of an eldest son' (replica).

His story had its true beginning not in his birth at the royal palace of Woodstock in the summer of 1330 but in the dark days of the reign of his grandfather, the fecklessly self-indulgent, stubbornly weak Edward II. Edward's queen, Isabella of France, a woman of strong and unattractive character, bore him four children and a pitiless grudge for spurning her in

11

favour of male bedfellows, the latest of whom was Hugh Despenser. His barons resented and rebelled against the privileges that he lavished on his favourites. The Commons despised him for his shameful defeat at Bannockburn by the bare-breeched Scottish barbarians under their Norman overlords.

Queen Isabella had early in life dramatically set her face against adultery. At the age of seventeen, on a visit to her father's court in Paris, she observed and denounced the extra-marital activities of two of her sisters-in-law, as a result of which the women were immured in fortresses, where one was smothered to death between two mattresses, and their lovers were flayed alive. But in 1325, after a dozen years of second-best marriage to Edward II (their fourth and final child was born in the summer of 1321), she escaped with her elder son to France, to join the 'tall, dark-complexioned, strong and well-built' Roger Mortimer, Baron of Wigmore. When Edward ordered her to return she replied that 'marriage is a coupling of man and woman ... Somebody has come between my husband and me, trying to break this union ... I shall not return until this intruder has been removed ... I shall assume the garments of widowhood and mourning until I am avenged.'

It was a scandalously merry widowhood. She lived in open adultery and delight with Mortimer, while collecting around her a group of influential malcontents that included her husband's brother, Edmund Earl of Kent. In the spring of 1326 she affianced her son Edward to Count William of Hainault's daughter Philippa, in return for an advance on the girl's dowry, with which she hired soldiers and ships. In the last week of September 1326 she landed in the Orwell estuary and, meeting no opposition from Edward's disgruntled subjects, marched by way of Bury St Edmunds and Cambridge towards London.

Learning that the king had retreated to Gloucester, she swung her army through Baldock, Dunstable and Oxford in pursuit. Edward ran once more, towards Hugh Despenser's palatinate of Glamorgan. Hugh's father, the Earl of Winchester, had taken refuge in Bristol, but when the queen appeared before the walls neither the citizens nor the garrison would support him. He surrendered and was hanged. Edward, suddenly finding himself a hunted outcast, stumbled aimlessly away with a few companions. He took ship at Chepstow

fuper miferum ꝫ coutulaf e ualce ꝫ
laxate ſunt o͛s aie q̃ ruant iiſeruo ꝫ
clamalãt uoce magna diꝛtes ꝟn
dicimus te rẽ fili dõi uiui q̃ dignaꝰ

es nobir fingeãui tair iⱒ dici ꝫ tⱒ uoc
tis quã totum tm̃p ꝙ uiuimus
tẽ tuã. ui ergo qui tuiꝛo duit dic lõ̃rã
qui ꝛpi lieuir ꝓtẽ ui ſcis i ſciã ſcloꝛ.

*The coronation of twenty-three-year-old Edward II in 1307. The Archbishop of Canterbury is holding the crown with his left hand, the Archbishop of York with his right.*

apparently attempting to get to Lundy Island, another of the Despensers' domains. He was blown back to Cardiff, where he disembarked, struggled westward and was finally captured at Neath Abbey on 16 November.

With him was taken Hugh Despenser. 'The said gentleman ... was brought before the Queen and all the barons and knights ... and sentenced ... to death and execution ... First he was dragged on a hurdle, with horns and trumpets from street to street, through all the town of Hereford, and then he was taken to a large square in the middle of the town where

13

all the people were assembled. There he was tied to a tall ladder so that all could see him, and they had made in that square a great fire. When he was thus bound they first cut off his male member and his testicles because he was a heretic and a sodomite, so it was said, and even with the King himself, for the King had driven out the Queen at his encitement. When his male member and testicles had been cut off they were thrown into the fire and burned; afterwards his belly was split open and his heart taken out and thrown into the fire to burn, because he was false-hearted and a traitor ... Afterwards ... his head was cut off and sent to London, and then he was hewn into four quarters which were sent to the four greatest cities of England after London.'

The king was held prisoner at Kenilworth. There on 20 January 1327, accepting the inevitable, he abdicated in favour of his son, who had already been acclaimed as Edward III by Parliament at Westminster and by the mob in the City of London. Just before Easter the ex-king was moved to Berkeley Castle in Gloucestershire where he was murdered on 21 September, in secrecy and with a barbaric cruelty intended to complement the punishment wreaked on Hugh Despenser.

The new king, a little over fourteen years old, was provided with a council to administer the realm until he came of age. Its members were largely supporters of Mortimer and the queen, who a year later fulfilled her bargain with William of Hainault by marrying her son to his daughter, the thirteen-year-old Philippa, on 24 January 1328. Mortimer appropriated the Despenser estates and inveigled the somewhat simple Edmund of Kent into believing that Edward II was still alive – and had him beheaded when he began to plot a restoration. The weathercocks of envy and anxiety swung again. Those who had rebelled against the king's favourite now grew restive under the queen's. They urged young Edward to assert himself against the upstart Mortimer.

Edward had sufficient grounds for fear and resentment – the public calumny and murder of his father, the almost contemptuous disregard with which his mother and Mortimer governed the country over his head, the increasing probability that he would share the fate of his father and his uncle Edmund. He knew that there was considerable public feeling against

14

Edward II and
Edward III on the
choir screen of
York Minster.

Mortimer for failing to deal firmly with Scottish border raids
and for accepting humiliating peace terms from both the Scots
and the French. Yet his sixteenth and seventeenth birthdays
passed and still he made no move.

In the summer of 1330, the court was at the royal manor
of Woodstock, where Henry I had constructed a park, 'walled
about with stone, seven miles in compass, and ... placed
therein, besides great store of deer, divers strange beasts, such

15

Edward of
Woodstock's Privy
Seal as Earl of
Chester.

as . . . lions, leopards, linces, porpentines and such other'. It was
here, on Friday 15 June, that Philippa gave birth to their first
child, 'a very fair, lusty and well-formed infant', whom they
christened Edward. It was the birth of this son that brought
the young king to the moment of decision – perhaps because
parenthood made the bonds of tutelage more obviously irk-
some; perhaps because he saw that the arrival of this new
generation of Plantagenets made it likely that Mortimer would
strike quickly. On 19 October 1330, when Parliament
assembled at Nottingham, Edward's supporters entered the

castle through a secret passage and, after a running fight, over-powered Mortimer in Isabella's room. He was impeached, found guilty of encompassing the late king's death, drawn on a hurdle to the scaffold like a felon, and hanged. Isabella's adulterous relations with him were not mentioned at the trial, but he was accused of sowing discord between her and her husband, 'making her believe that if she went to him he would kill her with a poignard or other weapon' so that 'the Queen never went to her Lord (to afford him her bed) to the great dishonour of the King and the whole Realm'. With her husband's reputation thus partially restored and her own no further tarnished, Isabella went into retirement on an allowance of £1,000 a year. Edward III was king at last, a tall, handsome young man, just eighteen.

The baby prince was taken to see his formidable grandmother at her favourite residence, Castle Rising, in November 1331. On 16 June 1332, the day after his second birthday, his sister Isabella was born. She shared his governess, the Lady Elizabeth, wife of William Saint-Omer, Steward of the Prince's Household, but was provided with a personal 'rocker', the damsel Joanna Gaunbun, whose wages were a lavish £10 a year. Just before his third birthday, on 18 March 1333, the young Edward was created Earl of Chester, and in that capacity, when he was five, he was ordered by his father to attend to the garrison and guard of the castles in his county and those of Flint and Rhuddlan. The Welsh needed watching while Edward dealt with the Scots. With a brilliant victory at Halidon Hill on 19 July 1333, Edward avenged his father's defeat at Bannockburn; the Scottish king, David Bruce, who was married to Edward's sister Joanna, fled for safety to the court of France. Philippe VI of France sent a fleet to support the Scottish ships that preyed on English merchantmen and threatened English ports, and, when Edward again went north in 1335, the possibility of French raids in his absence prompted him to have the Earl of Chester moved from Peterborough, where he had spent July at the abbey with Isabella and a new sister Joanna, to the safety of Nottingham Castle. The hazard passed, but the hatred between the Kings of England and France increased as Edward prepared to lay legal claim to the French throne.

The young King Edward III (*left*) is met outside Amiens by Philippe VI of France, to whom
he has come to pay homage – June 1329.

Philippe IV of France had had three sons who succeeded each other – Louis X (whose posthumous only son, Jean, lived less than a month), Philippe V and Charles IV – and one daughter, Isabella, who married Edward II and outlived all her brothers. When Charles IV died, his cousin, Philippe IV's brother's son, succeeded as Philippe VI. Edward III maintained that he had a better claim through his mother, daughter of Philippe IV; Philippe VI replied that in French law succession was restricted to the unbroken male line. Edward did not dispute the fact that a woman could not occupy the throne, but he asserted that she could nevertheless transmit the claim from grandfather to grandson. She could not be a sovereign, but she could be the 'plank or bridge' that led to sovereignty. It was indeed on a similar argument that two of his predecessors had successfully claimed the throne of England: Stephen, through his mother, daughter to William the Conqueror, and Henry II, founder of the Plantagenet–Angevin line, through Maud, daughter of Henry I.

Edward's case was embarrassed by his having recognized Philippe VI as King of France by doing homage to him as Duke of Aquitaine in 1329 and again in 1331. It is probable that he did not himself believe in the claim; but that he put it forward solely as a means of protecting his inheritance in France – the duchy of Aquitaine – from further encroachment by the French kings. It provided a pretext to ease the conscience of the Holy Roman Emperor, Ludwig of Bavaria – who was Edward's brother-in-law, having married Queen Philippa's sister – and Ludwig's vassal dukes and counts and margraves on France's northern frontiers with whom Edward signed a defensive and offensive alliance in the summer of 1337.

Philippe declared Edward's lands in France forfeit because of 'the many excesses, rebellions and acts of disobedience committed against us and our royal majesty by the King of England, Duke of Aquitaine'. War clouds thickened above the Channel. About Midsummer Day a comet was seen in the south-west of France, 'its tail and rays extending towards the east and north', which people took to be 'an omen of tribulations and wars to come'. (Though in England its influence turned out to be entirely beneficial, for 'anon there followed ... good chepe and wondrous great plenty ... in so much that a quarter of wheat

19

at London was sold for 2s, and good fatte oxe at a noble'.)
Edward published a manifesto setting out his grievances against
Philippe; Philippe's men captured Guernsey; Edward sent a
letter of defiance to Philippe, formally adopted the title of King
of France and appointed the Duke of Brabant as his lieutenant
with authority to take possession of the realm of France.

Pope Benedict XII, horrified at the prospect of Christians
committing the sin of killing each other, sent two cardinals to
beg Philippe and Edward to gain honour, glory and a reward
in the life to come by slaughtering Saracens instead. But Philippe was out of humour with the pope for postponing an earlier
crusade, and Edward distrusted him because he was a Frenchman, Jacques Fournier, formerly Bishop of Mirepoix. The
cardinals, Peter Gomez and Bertrand de Montfavence, reached
Paris in August 1337, and London at the end of the year. The
great procession of dignitaries that rode out to meet them at
Southwark – the Archbishop of Canterbury, six bishops, the
mayor and aldermen – also included a boy of seven, the king's
eldest son, who since February had held the title of Duke of
Cornwall – the first duchy ever to be erected in England,
though English kings had held the titles of Duke of Normandy
and Duke of Aquitaine.

Because he was a king's son, his upbringing had some unusual
aspects: the formal public reception of the cardinals, for instance, or the ceremonial, scarcely-comprehended council
meetings with the stewards and comptrollers of his extensive
estates. But for the most part he followed the same path to manhood as any other boy of good family. His first seven years he
spent in his mother's care, with his sisters Isabella and Joanna
as playmates, briefly joined by a brother, William of Windsor,
who died in babyhood and was succeeded by William of Hat-
field, who did not live much longer. A more interesting companion was his second cousin and foster-sister Joan, whom he
called Jeanette. Two years his senior, she was adopted by
Queen Philippa after Jeanette's gullible father, Edmund of
Kent, was tricked by Mortimer into double treason and
death.

The second seven years of his life he should, according to custom, have spent in the household of his father's overlord.
Edward had no overlord (not even as Duke of Aquitaine, since
he refused to accept Philippe as King of France). The boy was
therefore trained at his father's court with thirty or forty sons
of the greatest magnates of England. Among these he found
lifelong friends such as William Montagu, son of the Earl of
Salisbury, governor of the royal manor of Woodstock, and
Simon, kinsman of the wise Dr Burley who was almoner to
Queen Philippa and was appointed as one of the prince's tutors
as soon as he was old enough 'to learne his boke'. He still saw
much of Jeanette and his sisters, for he had not yet entirely left
the women's hall. It was their task to teach him the knightly
virtues of polite behaviour and service to others without loss
of pride, to observe the ten commandments and the twelve
articles of faith, and to avoid the seven deadly sins – until, growing taller and stronger, he began to wrestle and race on foot
and horse and, at the age of fourteen, passed entirely into the
world of men, graduating from page to squire.

In April 1338, a second ominous comet was observed trailing
fire across Europe. In July instructions were given for residents
on the south coast to take refuge in fortresses in the event of
an invasion, or alternatively to retire with all their movable
property to at least ten miles inland. The king meanwhile
sailed for Antwerp, leaving the Duke of Cornwall with the title
of Guardian of England. Lady Saint-Omer, the Mistress of the
King's Children, had surrendered her eldest charge to Sir
Nicholas de la Beche, Master of the Prince's Household and
Constable of the Tower. It was at the Tower that the prince
officially resided until his father's return.

Edward's Flemish allies were unwilling to give him full support without a more definite commitment from the emperor,
so he journeyed on into the Rhineland to Coblenz, where the
emperor appointed him his vicar and commander of the feudal
levies of the Low Countries for a period of seven years. But
Edward was still not ready to launch a major war on France.
In the first year of his reign he had, at the dictation of his mother
and Mortimer, confirmed the forty-year-old Statute of Winchester under which 'no man be compelled to go out of his
county except from necessity because of the sudden coming of

strange enemies into the realm'. If the king wished to engage in foreign ventures he must pay the men who fought for him either from the revenues of the royal estates or from taxes specially voted by the Lords and Commons in Parliament and the clergy in Convocation. Parliament was not yet convinced of the need to support the king, who for the moment must finance his war out of his own purse, though he managed to increase his income by entering into a wool monopoly with the leading merchants.

Philippe sent his French troops marching into Gascony and his hired Genoese to raid Southampton, following this up during the winter and spring with attacks on ports from Harwich round to Bristol, burning Plymouth, Hastings and Rye. On 23 October 1338, 'Edward, Duke of Cornwall and Earl of Chester, our most dear son, Guardian of England', transmitted his father's orders to the mayor, aldermen and sheriffs of London: 'that you cause the city to be closed, and fortified against hostile attacks towards the water, with stone or with board, and that you cause piles to be driven across the water for the defence of the city aforesaid.' The young prince that year also held a Parliament at Northampton.

In Antwerp, on 29 November, Queen Philippa gave birth to another son, whom Edward named Lionel as a compliment to the Duke of Brabant, whose badge was a lion. To pay for the recruitment of his reluctant allies' armies – and the cost of his own board and lodgings – the English king borrowed money from Rhenish and Tuscan bankers, raised loans on his jewellery from Flemish and Brabantine merchants, and pawned his gold crown to Baldwin, Archbishop of Treves. (Later the queen's gold crown and another smaller one were similarly pledged.) 'We should have been dishonoured forever and our kingdom put in peril had not a friend lent us money on the promise that he should receive some wool,' Edward had written to the prince in August; and in February 1339 he tried to cement one alliance without money by arranging the prince's marriage to the Duke of Brabant's daughter, Margaret, 'within one year after he shall be old enough' – a project that was soon forgotten in the changing political dispositions. In July 1339 Edward sent a letter to the pope, setting out his title to the French throne (arguing that his claim was exactly parallel to that of Jesus to the throne of

David, through Mary who could not exercise it but could pass it on). That month French ships attacked Sandwich but were chased back across the Channel and Boulogne was burned in revenge; the Earl of Derby raided Le Tréport. In September Edward moved his motley army forward into Hainault and on the 20th launched them across the border and through the French-dominated Cambrésis.

It was a brief and inglorious campaign. The Counts of Hainault and Namur turned back at the French frontier, belatedly deciding that they could not fight against Philippe, from whom they held some territories in fief. The remainder of Edward's forces were confronted by a French army at La Flamengerie on Friday 22 October. 'At vespers three spies were taken,' Edward wrote in a letter to his son, 'and were examined, each one separately, and they all agreed that Philippe would give us battle on Saturday and that he was a league and a half from us. On the Saturday we were on the field a full quarter before daybreak and took up our position to fight ... In the meantime, one of our scouts, a Knight of Germany, was taken, who had seen all our array and perhaps revealed it all to the enemy, so that they at once withdrew their vanguard and gave orders to camp, and made trenches around them, and cut down big trees, to prevent our approaching them.' Since Philippe refused battle and Edward's allies – partly because of a shortage of food – were unwilling to penetrate further into France, the two armies turned about and went home.

This fiasco marked the end of hostilities. Edward returned to Antwerp for Christmas, and from there sent renewed demands for money to Parliament – which had adjourned in October without replying to his earlier requests. In the last week of January 1340 Edward had himself proclaimed King of France in the market place at Ghent, dated an edict 'in the first year of our reign over France and the fourteenth over England', and on his coat of arms quartered the lilies of France with the lions of England. On hearing of this, Pope Benedict XII wrote to condemn him for being 'led by perverse and fraudulent counsel into courses neither expedient nor seemly', but neither Edward nor his bishops had much respect for the pope's opinions. On 20 February he slipped away from Sluys to England leaving his queen as surety for his debts.

23

January 1340.
Edward inspects his
new coat of arms,
on which the lilies
of France are
quartered with the
lions of England.

He was not long at home. From the Parliament that he recon-
vened on 29 March 1340, he received a tax of one-ninth and
of forty shillings on every sack of wool exported. (Taxes were
commonly one-tenth or one-fifteenth of the value of all movable
property, collected from shires and boroughs on an assessment
that was unchanged through most of the reign.) In return he
confirmed the disputed right of Parliament to be consulted on
all taxation and promised to rectify various infringements of
the laws by sheriffs, purveyors and other royal servants. Soon
after Whitsun he had assembled an army of 4,000 men-at-arms
and 12,000 archers around the mouth of the Orwell, with 200
ships to carry them across the North Sea.

Just as he was ready to sail, word came that the French had
marshalled a large fleet, with reinforcements from Spain, at
Sluys, the town where great sluices regulated the waters of the
canal to Bruges, and which in those days overlooked a vast
harbour stretching from Blankenberge to Cadzand. Edward

24

ordered another sixty ships to be brought round from the Cinque Ports and, two days before Midsummer Day, sailed eastward. By the following evening he was off Blankenberge, in sight of the barrier formed by the French vessels, lashed together in three lines or 'battles', as they might have been arrayed for defence in depth on dry land: 'A full, huge and boisterous navy of divers nations ... So great a number of ships that their masts seemed to be like a great wood.' Edward ordered his own ships to drop anchor and wait for morning.

There was little to be done in the way of manoeuvring. The French had a numerical superiority of four to one. When the dawn broke, Edward circled to the south-west so as to preserve the advantage of the wind that had brought him over from England without incurring the penalty of getting the morning sun in his men's eyes. He 'set all his ships in order, the greatest before, well furnished with archers, and ever between two ships of archers he had one ship with men-at-arms; and then he made another battle to lie aloof, with archers to comfort ever them that were most weary if need were. And there were a great number of countesses, ladies, knights' wives and other damosels, that were going to see the Queen at Gaunt: these ladies the King caused to be well kept with three hundred men-at-arms and five hundred archers.' At nine o'clock he gave the signal to attack. 'A terrible shout rose from the whole line of ships; a hail of arrows and bolts from crossbows slew thousands ... Many had their brains dashed out by stones thrown from the turrets.'

The Spanish war-galleys and the great ship *Christopher* (in which Edward had sailed to Antwerp and which the French had captured from the English in the previous September) were so high out of the water that Edward's men-at-arms had difficulty in using their 'great hooks and grapples of iron' to board them under the covering barrage of arrows. 'This battle was right fierce and terrible; for the battles on the sea are more dangerous than the battles by land; for on the sea there is no recoiling nor fleeing; there is no remedy but to fight and abide fortune, and every man to show his prowess.' Having grappled, they set to work 'hand to hand, with spears, axes and swords ... At last the French were defeated and driven out of the first group of ships and the English took control of them ... Then

The Battle of Sluys.

they turned their hands to the second group and with great difficulty made the attack. But once this was launched the second line was cleared more easily than the first, for most of the Frenchmen quit the ships and jumped into the sea.'

Weary and with the light fading, Edward's men waited till morning to assault the final line of French ships. During the night, thirty of these slipped away. The remainder were soon taken. 'The number of ships of war that were captured was about 200, with 30 barges; the number of the enemy that were slain and drowned was about 25,000, and of Englishmen about 4,000.' It was a resounding victory for Edward, a staggering reverse for Philippe. 'So many French and Normans were drowned there that it was said of them in mockery that if God had given the gift of speech to the fish of the sea, from thence forward they would have spoken French because they had eaten so many.' The king received the congratulations of his Flemish allies, made a pilgrimage of thanksgiving to Our Lady of Aardenburg and then rode on to Ghent where, three months before, Queen Philippa had given birth to yet another son, named John of Gaunt after his birthplace.

In July Edward once more set out from his base at Vilvoorde, with an army estimated at 100,000 men, to besiege Tournai, while Robert of Artois (whose claim to the county under the Salic Law was supported by Edward and denied by the court of France) headed for Saint-Omer with 50,000. (Contemporary figures are wildly distorted. Though they may occasionally be understated in order to emphasize a triumph of David over Goliath, it is usually fair to assume that they have been exaggerated by two, three or four times. In this instance they are the ones given by Edward to his Parliament.) Artois was beaten off; Edward failed to reduce Tournai. By the second week of September Philippe brought an army to Bouvines, seven or eight miles away, but showed no eagerness to attack. Edward's allies, some of them loath to confront their liege lord on the field of battle, others tired of waiting for their pay, began to drift away home. The widowed Countess of Hainault, who was Philippe's sister and Edward's mother-in-law and who had become a Cistercian abbess, brought the two disputants together in a lonely chapel at Esplechin, just south of Tournai, where they agreed to a truce until June the following year.

The campaign had been another disappointment to Edward, another source of shame for Philippe – but no surprise to French moralists. 'Men were now beginning to wear the most unseemly costumes. This was true of noblemen in particular, knights, squires and their followers, but it was true to some extent of the burgesses and of nearly all servants. Garments were short to the point of indecency ... and everybody began to grow long beards ... Men thus apparelled were more likely to flee in the face of the enemy, as was afterwards many times proved.'

Certainly the French had shown little appetite for war, and Edward could justifiably complain that he was having more trouble from friend than foe. His allies were deserting him because he could not pay them; and he could not pay them because his subjects were withholding the taxes that Parliament had voted him in April. He wrote to his ministers, urging them to redouble their efforts. In July the Duke of Cornwall summoned Parliament again with the familiar warning: 'No earl or baron may attend armed with his sword. Children from the neighbourhood are forbidden to gather within the precincts of the Palace of Westminster to play prisoner's base or other improper games, such as knocking off people's hats.' In this calm atmosphere Parliament sympathized with the king's complaints, but seemed unable to compel his subjects to pay their dues.

At the end of November 1340 the king suddenly appeared in person and in a raging temper. He had again been forced to slip away from his creditors by a subterfuge. Pretending that he was merely taking Queen Philippa to the coast for a change of air, he got into a ship at Sluys and set sail for the Thames. On arrival in the early hours of the morning at the Tower of London, the fortress at the heart of his realm, he found not a single sentry on duty. He promptly put the constable, Nicholas de la Beche, under arrest with several members of his council, and appointed the lord chamberlain, Bartholomew de Burghersh, as Master of the Prince's Household in place of La Beche.

That winter the king sent special commissioners throughout his kingdom to collect the overdue taxes. They met with resistance, especially in London. When Parliament assembled in the late spring of 1341 it refused to release more funds until the king had confirmed various ancient and neglected charters and undertaken that officers of state – chancellor, chamberlain, treasurers, chief justices and so on – should be appointed with the advice of Parliament, that they should take their oaths of office in the presence of Parliament and that their conduct would be examined by each new Parliament. Edward's war looked like costing him a good deal more than he expected. On top of this came the news that the emperor had cancelled Edward's vicariate and come to terms with his uncle, Philippe of France.

On 4 June 1341 (the day before Edward's eighth child, Edmund, was born at King's Langley) David of Scotland landed at Inverbervie in Kincardine, supported by French soldiers. Edward moved north to take command of his troops at Newcastle, having candidly informed his sheriffs that he was determined to repeal 'the pretended statute of the last Parliament ... As our rejecting it would have dissolved Parliament in discord, without any business having been transacted, and so all our arduous negotiations would have been ruined, we dissembled and allowed the pretended statute to be sealed.' In January 1342 he signed a truce with his brother-in-law David and returned to London to continue his preparations against France. In October he once more appointed his eldest son Guardian of England and sailed to Brittany with reinforcements for the troops he had already sent under the Earls of Northampton, Derby and Oxford. There he was supporting Jean de Montfort who was disputing the title of duke with Philippe's nominee, Charles of Blois.

It was a cold, wet, blustery, unproductive winter. Early in December the young Duke of Cornwall received a letter from his father with the usual instructions to 'stir up our Chancellor and Treasurer to send us money'. The king was expediently optimistic. 'Dear Son, know that ... we have laid siege to the city of Vannes, which is the best town of Brittany after the town of Nantes and can best compel and restrain the country to our obedience ... We hope, by the power of God, to have a good issue, for since our coming into these parts he has given us a good beginning.' But the city did not surrender. Edward's soldiers, under orders not to antagonize the native population, fought glumly in filthy weather and with no hope of loot. After yet another inconclusive campaign Edward signed a fresh truce at Malestroit in January 1343 and returned to England in March.

He was short of money again, and had to summon Parliament to ask for it. It was the first time he had faced them since

Edward III (*right*) agrees on a truce with his brother-in-law, David II of Scotland, in January 1342.

the 'pretended statute' of 1341. He prepared the way by sending the lord chamberlain, Bartholomew de Burghersh, to explain to them that 'because this war was undertaken and begun by the common assent of the Prelates, Magnates and Commons, the King did not wish to make peace without their common assent'. They were suitably flattered. They approved the king's decision to treat for peace and assured him that if he could not obtain honourable terms 'they would aid him to maintain his quarrel with all their might'. It was a promise that delighted him. They failed to persuade him to withdraw his repudiation of the act of 1341, but he readily agreed to set up a commission of inquiry into the increased lawlessness in the kingdom over the past two years.

The disappointing results of the foreign affrays – and an admitted increase in crimes of violence – had led to widespread criticism of the modern provocative, permissive behaviour and dress. The Archbishop of Canterbury complained that priests were failing to wear clerical clothing and walking the streets 'with an outer habit very short and tight-fitting ..., with long beards, rings on their fingers, and girdled belts studded with precious stones of wonderful size ..., their boots of red and green, peaked and cut in many ways'. In this they were merely following their flock, for, said the scolding voice of another cleric, it was notorious that 'Englishmen ... changed them every year divers shapes and disguising of clothing, of long, large and wide clothes, deserting from all honest and good usage; and another time short clothes, narrow-waisted, jagged-edged ... and hoods overlong and large, and overmuch hanging that, if I shall speak the truth, they were more like to tormentors and devils than men in their clothing and appearance and other array'. The women, of course, luring the weaker sex into sin, 'more dreadfully surpassed the men in array and curiouslier; for they were so strait-clothed that they let hang fox-tails sewed beneath their clothes for to conceal and hide their arse; the which disguising and pride peradventure afterward brought forth and caused many mishaps and mischiefs in the realm of England'.

Edward's remedy for this supposed decadence was to encourage an interest in the martial arts among his earls, barons, knights and commoners. He provided them with exercise and

A sign of the times – the priest is confined to the stocks with one of his flock.

entertainment in a series of jousts, tournaments and hastiludes in London, Nottingham and Windsor. This was no pantomime fighting. In January 1344 the Earl of Salisbury, Marshal of England, a famous warrior in Scotland and France and father of the Duke of Cornwall's friend, William Montagu, died of wounds received in the tournament at Windsor. It was on this occasion that Edward announced his intention of reviving Arthurian glories by instituting a Round Table of three hundred knights. The following month he ordered carpenters and masons to be engaged – probably to rebuild the Norman Round Tower at Windsor to provide a fit setting for his Round Table. But later he decided on a smaller, more select company, which may have held its first meeting on 23 April that year – the feast of St George. It was this Order of St George that was to develop into the Order of the Garter, the oldest and most distinguished secular confraternity of chivalry in England and the world.

Arthur's Round Table had accommodated 150 knights and Edward had originally intended to found an order of twice as many. He now decided to restrict it to two sets of twelve (the

number that the ancient Round Table at Winchester had been constructed for) with himself at the head of one dozen and his eldest son at the head of the other. They would compete in loyalty to the crown as they did in the exercise of arms. In the stalls of the chapel that he proposed building in honour of St George at Windsor, they would confront each other in prayer as they did in the lists.

It was heady stuff for a boy who had just entered his teens. Over and over again he had heard recited and sung the stories of the classic days of chivalry, the great crusades, the silver-misted legends of the adventurous knights at Arthur's court; and, like every boy in every age, he had believed them lost for ever. Yet here was his handsome, tempestuous, gallant father reviving them in all their colour, their courage, their high ideals. The effect that they made on the young prince's impressionable mind guided and gilded his actions throughout the harsh time in which he lived and the often brutal incidents in which he was involved.

He had surrendered his guardianship of England upon his father's return to England in March 1343. Almost his last

Par dieu fait li baudrains / oz vos va ricement

on truet uier / au roi qui ne ment mie

*Above*  Jousting: a sport in which injuries were often serious and sometimes fatal.

font en fa opaigne · x · mille chenalier

*Right*  The education of a squire, who was taught to play chess and draughts ...

... as well as to practise his skill with a lance against the quintain on foot and on a wooden horse ...

ue il nes honneurt ainfi q fere doit

folfe font parfont ꝫ li terrail font droit

... and finally in
full armour on
a real charger

official duty, a few weeks before that, had been to consult the
chancellor about raising money 'for the burial of the Lady
Blanche, my sister', whose birth is unrecorded but probably
took place in the second half of 1342. (The total number of
Philippa's children is unknown, but she quite possibly had one a
year for at least the first eighteen years of her marriage – a dozen
names are recorded during that period, and another in 1354.)
On 12 May 1343, in the presence of Parliament, his father had
bestowed on him the title of Prince of Wales, investing him with
a coronet, a gold ring and a silver rod.

Now that he had graduated from page to squire, his education was concerned with essentially masculine affairs, hawking,
hunting, horsemanship, skill at arms with sword and lance and
the short-handled cavalry mace and maul and axe – although,
since the perfect knight was courteous and amorous as well as
bellicose, he was encouraged to cultivate his singing voice and
his aptitude to set little verses to little tunes, or to pass an hour
at draughts or chess or backgammon. The next great step in
his career would be the moment when his father spoke the
solemn words 'I make you a knight' and buckled a sword round
his waist, while two squires fastened spurs to his heels. In normal
times this would not happen until he was twenty-one.

35

Chapter Two

# 𝔖𝔴𝔬𝔯𝔡 𝔞𝔫𝔡 𝔖𝔭𝔲𝔯𝔰

These were far from normal times. In France the House of Valois was continuing the consolidation of power that had begun under Philippe-Auguste and the saintly, humble, infinitely obdurate Louis IX a century before. The purpose was to strengthen the central government of the king by breaking the grip and spirit of his great vassals. Of these, the greatest had been the English Angevin kings. Their empire had included as much land in France as in England; the three lions, *passant guardant*, on the English royal standard were in fact the single *lions léopardés* of Normandy, Maine and Aquitaine. But Normandy had gone, and Maine, and more than half of Aquitaine, and still the French kings continued to nibble and claw, squeeze and twist. Because of this ceaseless encroachment on their lands and those of their tenants, both Edward I and Edward II had been forced into war with France. Now, to save the remains of his continental inheritance, Edward III was forced into war as well – though it is true that he required little compulsion.

On 1 January 1346 he ordered ships to be assembled at Portsmouth to take him to France at Candlemas; at Candlemas (2 February) he put it off until mid-Lent; in March, because of the stormy weather, it was postponed until Easter. How much of this was merely intended to deceive Philippe's spies is difficult to assess; when Edward at last arrived at Porchester at the beginning of June, the news got swiftly to Philippe, who sent a warning to the Scots to be ready to invade England. That same day, 20 June, Edward appointed Sir Hugh Hastings, son of a former Seneschal of Aquitaine, as his lieutenant in the Low Countries, while letting it be known that he was leading most of his expedition (rumour estimated the number of ships at between 600 and 1,500) to Gascony, where he had already sent a small army under his cousin, Henry of Lancaster.

For nearly a year past, commissioners of array had been reviewing all men between sixteen and sixty in each county and selecting the best to serve in the army. It was every Englishman's duty, established by Henry II's Assize of Arms in 1181 and confirmed by Edward I's Statute of Winchester in 1285, to provide himself with basic arms and armour – from the poor man's pike or bow to the yeoman's hauberk, helmet, sword, dagger and horse. Their pay, ranging from 2d to 6d a day, was charged to the king if he summoned them to accompany him abroad. But on this occasion, by the consent of Parliament, he demanded that 'from every person who had a hundred shillings in rent he might have one [foot] archer to go abroad with him, and from those having ten marks a hobbler (mounted on a light horse or hobby), and from those having twenty marks one man-at-arms'. Their ranks were swollen by men seeking an amnesty from crimes – and most importantly by the retinues of well-known warriors who contracted to serve the king for agreed wages over a set period and with a stated number of knights, men-at-arms and archers both mounted and on foot.

Exactly how many men were brought to the banks of the Solent and Southampton Water is impossible to say. Contemporary assessments vary from 14,000 to 85,000. A modern estimate is 16,000. If this is correct, the king may have required 1,000 ships to transport both men and horses. (When Henry of Lancaster sailed to Gascony the year before, 152 ships, with crews of 148 masters, 44 constables – mates or boatswains – 2,380 seamen and 295 boys, were needed to transport the force of 500 men-at-arms, 500 mounted archers, 500 foot archers and 500 Welsh infantrymen. The average seems to have been a crew of twenty, a cargo of fifteen men, plus horses and stores.) With this great invasion fleet, Edward put out of Portsmouth harbour early in July – not eastward for Flanders or westward round Finistère to Gascony but due south, to open another front in Normandy. With him, one month past his sixteenth birthday, went the Prince of Wales.

On 12 July 1346, after being blown off course and riding at anchor for several days against contrary winds off the coast of

Every man was obliged by law to provide himself with a weapon and take part in regular practice.

Cornwall, the fleet sailed down the Cotentin peninsula to the small port of Saint-Vaast-la-Hougue. As he set foot on French soil the king tripped and, to the horror of his companions, fell face downward, 'so rudely that the blood brast out of his nose'. It was a deeply disturbing omen.

The knights who helped him to his feet begged him: 'Sir, for God's sake enter again into your ship, and come not to land this day, for this is but an evil sign for us.' But the quick-witted king replied, '"This is a good token for me, for the land desireth to have me." Of the which answer all his men were right joyful.' It was much the same remark as his great-great-great-great-great-great-grandfather had made when he stumbled on the beach at Pevensey before defeating Harold.

He set up his tented headquarters along the shore and during the next five days completed the disembarkation of his army, marshalled it into three 'battles' – vanguard, centre and rear-guard – and, as was customary at the beginning of a campaign, knighted a large number of newly-appointed commanders and noble-born esquires, including his eldest son.

On 16 July the small force that the king had sent to Flanders under the command of Hugh Hastings reached its destination. Philippe of France was faced with war on four fronts: Gascony, Brittany, Normandy and Flanders. On the 17th Edward marched inland, captured Valognes the following day, turned south, burned Saint-Côme, crossed the Douve, accepted the surrender of Carentan, crossed the Vire and took Saint-Lô, most of whose terrified citizens had already fled. In Paris, Philippe sent out a summons to his great vassals to join him with their levies, wrote to David of Scotland, urging him to invade England, and rode to the abbey of Saint-Denis to raise the *oriflamme*, the long, forked orange banner of the Kings of France, the mere sight of which was said to strike infidels blind.

From Saint-Lô Edward swung eastward through Calvados to Caen and Lisieux. His fleet sailed parallel with him, capturing ships and plundering seaports. Ahead of him rode Geoffroi de Harcourt, Lord of Saint-Sauveur-le-Vicomte, who had been exiled from France on a charge of plotting to seize the duchy of Normandy from Philippe's eldest son, Jean. He had sought refuge first in Brabant and then in England and was now returned for revenge.

'He took 500 men-at-arms and 2,000 archers, quitted the King and his host and went a good six or seven leagues [fifteen to eighteen miles] before the host, burning and destroying. And they found the country rich and fertile in all things, the granaries full of corn, the houses full of all manner of riches . . ., lambs, sheep, pigs, calves, oxen, cows; they took them and carried them to the King's host, but they did not surrender to him the gold and silver that they found in great plenty, but kept it for themselves.'

While Harcourt ranged forward on the right flank, returning to the king's headquarters every day or two, another body of some 2,500 men under the Earl of Warwick was ravaging the territory on the seaward side. 'And the noble King of England and his son the Prince of Wales continued to lead their host forward by short stages, always finding lodgings between tierce [mid-morning] and mid-day, for they discovered the land to be so fertile that they had no need of provisions, save for wine, and even of that they found sufficient, for the people of the country had been taken unawares and had hidden nothing away. It was no wonder that they were astounded, for they had never known war, nor seen men under arms – yet now they saw men kill without pity, burn and rob houses, burn and lay waste the countryside.'

With panic horror sweeping before him, Edward advanced on Caen. There the Marshal Robert Bertrand, his brother, the

The ceremony of
knighthood was
sometimes lavish
and individual.

Bishop of Bayeux, the Chamberlain Lord of Tancarville, and
the Count of Eu, Constable of France, had rallied the chivalry
of Normandy with their retainers and mustered the town
militia. Edward launched his attack on Wednesday 26 July.
'They met with determined resistance on the part of the townspeople,' says one French account; but the Belgian canon Le
Bel claimed that 'as soon as these gentlemen of the town saw
the banner of the King of England and so many fine soldiers
the like of which they had never seen before, they were so afraid
that nobody in the world could have prevented their retreating
into the town, whether the constables and marshals wished it
or not'. Many of them took refuge in the fortress, leaving the
remainder to guard the vital bridge that linked the two halves
of the town and 'was much strengthened with a stockade and
portcullis'. Here certainly the French put up 'a strong battle
and long-during', but the town 'was badly walled and the river
was low, so that the English entered in many places and fell
upon the rear of the French who were fighting at the bridge'.

Tancarville and the Count of Eu escaped to the upper floors
of the gatehouse from which 'they perceived a gentle knight
who had but one eye, who was called Sir Thomas Holland, and
five or six good bachelors whom they had aforetime accompanied and encountered in campaigns in Prussia and Granada
... They called to them and begged them "Ho! for God's sake,
fair knights, come up and protect us from these merciless
men!"' So Holland, who had sworn to wear a white silk patch

40

over one eye 'until he had done some deed of arms in France', rescued his former comrades of crusades against the heathen Teutons and Moors, delighted to have such rich ransoms fall into his lap. The city was sacked, 'and each man saw before his eyes his mother and sister murdered, his wife and daughter violated, houses burned and robbed'. By the custom of war, the citizens of a town that failed to surrender when called upon forfeited all rights. Certainly many paid dearly for a decision that had been taken for them by their masters. 'A great number of knights and squires were slain, and other people of the city, in the streets and houses and gardens,' a cleric in the king's retinue wrote to Queen Philippa: 'It cannot be known what number of men of substance were slain, for they were presently stripped, so that they could not be recognized. And no gentleman was slain on our side save one squire who was wounded and died two days after.'

'Our fleet, which kept in touch with us, has burnt and laid waste the whole sea coast from Barfleur as far as the Fosse de Colleville near Caen,' the king wrote to the Archbishop of York on 30 July 1346, 'and likewise has burnt the town of Cherbourg and the ships of Le Havre, so that either by us or by our people there have been burnt one hundred or more great ships and other vessels of the enemy.'

Tancarville, Eu and the other notable prisoners were sent off to England to await ransoming. The towns of Bayeux and Lisieux, profiting from the sad lesson of Caen, surrendered without any attempt at resistance. Edward pursued his leisurely course eastward: 'about the bredth of 20 miles he wasted all manner of thing that he found.' Philippe hurried from Paris to Rouen to bar Edward's passage across the Seine. Edward, finding the bridge at Rouen broken (as a defensive measure, a section of the stone bridge on the side adjoining the city was built of wood, which could be easily dismantled or even burned), moved up the left bank of the Seine towards Paris. Philippe kept pace on the north bank, sending demolition groups ahead to destroy the bridges at Pont-de-l'Arche, Vernon, Meulan and Poissy, but 'although there were continuous pillagings and burnings throughout the whole region ... and up to a mile of him, yet he would not and dared not cross the waters of the Seine as he could have done, for the defence of

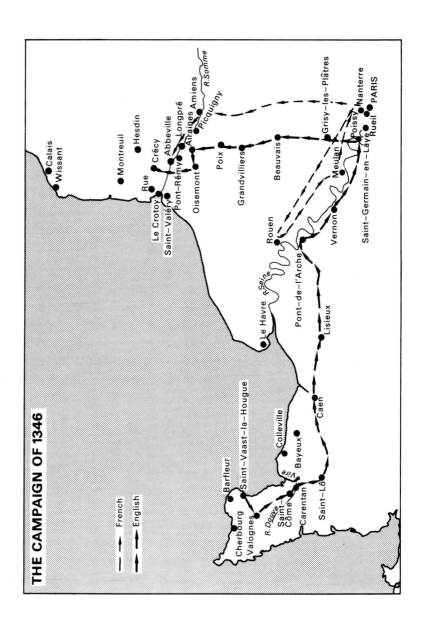

THE CAMPAIGN OF 1346

French

English

Calais
Wissant
Montreuil
Hesdin
Rue
Crécy
Abbeville
Longpré
Airaines
Amiens
R.Somme
Picquigny
Grisy-les-Plâtres
Nanterre
PARIS
Pont-Rémy
Poix
Rueil
Poissy
Le Crotoy
Saint-Valéry
Oisemont
Grandvilliers
Beauvais
Meulan
Saint-Germain-en-Laye
Vernon
Rouen
Pont-de-l'Arche
R.Seine
Le Havre
Lisieux
Caen
Colleville
Bayeux
Vire
Saint-Lô
Saint-Côme
Carentan
R.Douve
Barfleur
Saint-Vaast-la-Hougue
Cherbourg
Valognes

42

his people and his kingdom,' wrote Edward's chaplain Richard de Wynkeley. The chronicler Le Bel was even more scathing about the French king who 'has in all places kept himself so as to ease his person and keep from danger ... The less should be his praise and honour among all men.'

Although Edward was heading for Paris, he had no intention of attacking the French capital. He had not enough men either to take it or to hold it. He had laid a claim to the throne of France, but this was not the moment to enforce it: its value for the present was that it gave him a legalistic excuse for contesting Philippe's claim to be his overlord in Aquitaine and provided justification for rebellion by any other of Philippe's vassals whom he could win over. The real purpose of his invasion of France was simply to despoil the country. It was not an action of wanton spite or brutality; it was a gesture of defiance and provocation, to humiliate Philippe and to demonstrate to Philippe's subjects that their king was unable to fulil his obligation to protect them. 'The King of England marched to Saint-Germain-en-Laye, looted it, and burned the royal palace there,' wrote the head of the Carmelite order in France. 'The English also burned many nearby villages, such as Nanterre, La Chaussée, Rueil. They even burned the tower of Montjoie, which the King of France had rebuilt magnificently not long before. I who write this witnessed all these things, for they were to be seen from Paris by anybody who climbed up into a turret. The fires and the closeness of the English to Paris amazed and astonished everybody in the city, for nobody ever thought to see such a thing.' 'These were the principal residences and the special abodes of the King of France, which was a great dishonour to the kingdom,' added the monk of Saint-Denis who recorded it in the *Great Chronicles of France*.

Edward had made his point. He had dramatically humbled his opponent. But he had by now penetrated deep into hostile territory. Philippe had had a month in which to gather a force large enough to crush the English. On 14 August 1346 he sent a letter to Edward's headquarters in a convent at Poissy, belatedly challenging him to battle. Edward made no formal reply but he mentioned in the presence of Philippe's messenger, the Archbishop of Besançon, that he proposed marching to Montfort l'Amaury, a small town on the edge of the Forest of Rambouillet and on the road to Chartres. At the same time Edward ordered the Prince of Wales, who led the raids on the districts west of Paris, to push southward and westward, as if aiming to cross the Bièvre and cut upwards to the Seine east of Paris. To block this move, and to be well placed to pursue Edward if he made for Chartres, Philippe brought his army across the river to Antony, seven or eight miles south of the city walls.

The French began to take up their positions on Wednesday 16 August. During the night Edward's engineers had completed work on the bridge at Poissy which they had been secretly repairing for three days past. Edward threw across a heavy cavalry detachment under William de Bohun, Earl of Northampton, who swept aside the militia that Philippe had left to patrol the north bank. That evening Edward was in Grisy-les-Plâtres, more than twenty miles north-east of Paris. It was not until the following day that Philippe learned that Edward had slipped out of the cage.

Edward was marching north as fast as his booty-laden carts would comfortably allow – an average of twelve or thirteen miles a day. His intention was evidently to link up with Hugh Hastings and the Flemings who had crossed the Lys and were besieging Béthune. He skirted to the east of Beauvais, sending troops to burn its suburbs but wasting no time on trying to enter and sack the town. On 19 August, near Grandvilliers, his advance guard clashed with the troops of Philippe's ally, John of Luxemburg, King of Bohemia, whose sister had married Philippe's predecessor, Charles IV. Edward continued through Poix, making for the bridge across the Somme at Abbeville. He was following the line of the modern Route Nationale N.1 from Paris to Calais; Philippe, moving faster because he was not burdened with loot, had taken the Paris–Dunkirk road (N.16), and was at this moment in Amiens.

On 22 August, from his overnight headquarters at Airaines, seven miles south of the Somme, Edward sent out reconnaissance groups in a northern and eastern arc to Pont-Rémy, Longpré, Hangest, Picquigny. They returned with the news

that all the possible river crossings were guarded by local
levies – and 'that the King of France was in pursuit with a very
great host'. Philippe was in fact already advancing from
Amiens, and so close that, according to one chronicler, 'King
Edward left his dinner, which was already prepared, and departed in great haste with all his army; and the French came
to Airaines and found the dishes and ate their fill.'

With the bridges across the Somme denied to him, Edward
was now marching due west. He could be making for Le Tréport or the better harbour facilities at Dieppe. Whichever direction he chose, he had to gain sufficient time and room for
manoeuvre so that he could turn, marshal his strung-out forces
and fight off the French before they destroyed him piecemeal,
tail first. Already the peasants of Picardy were showing more
resistance than the inhabitants of the other areas he had passed
through. A series of running battles marked the advance – or
was it now an unmistakable retreat? – from Airaines to Oisemont. Edward's flanking squadrons set fire to so many farms
and barns that 'the sparks flew as far as Abbeville'. The citizens
of Oisemont marched out to challenge the invader, but discovered too late that rumour had exaggerated the English
king's weakness. They 'readily withdrew themselves and took
to flight, and there were a great number of them dead, drowned
and prisoners, and the town was taken and pillaged; and the
noble King lodged that night in the great hospice [of the
Knights of St John], wondering how he might make the crossing'. He was still seeking a way across the Somme.

His scouts had ridden the length of the river from Abbeville
to Saint-Valéry and taken many prisoners. These were brought
before the king, who 'right courteously demanded of them, if
there were any among them that knew any passage beneath
Abbeville, that he and his host might pass over the river
Somme'. One of them – 'a varlet called Gobin Agace' – succumbed to Edward's offer to waive ransom for himself and
twenty of his companions. 'Sir,' he replied, 'I promise you on
the jeopardy of my head I shall bring you to such a place ...
There be certain places in the passage that ye shall pass twelve
men afront two times between day and night: ye shall not go
in the water above the knees ... The passage is hard in the
bottom with white stones, so that all your carriage may go

45

surely; therefore the passage is called Blanche-Taque.' 'The King of England slept not much that night, for at midnight he arose and sowned his trumpet: then incontinent they made ready carriages and all things, and at the breaking of the day they departed.'

The ford at Blanche-Taque ran from the hamlet of Saigneville on the south bank of the Somme to what is now a cart-track, still known as the Route des Valois, below the N.40a downstream from Port-le-Grand. Edward's vanguard arrived at Saigneville soon after sun-up on St Bartholomew's Day, but the tide was still too high for them to cross. By the time the white streak which gave the ford its name was visible, the northern bank was occupied by enemy troops – probably 4,000 men of the Picardy militia under Godemar du Fay, commander of the French armies on the frontiers of Flanders and Hainault. Meanwhile Philippe of France was advancing along the southern bank, satisfied that he had Edward cornered.

Edward ordered his advance guard to cross. Northampton and Warwick trotted their men-at-arms to mid-stream, then lumbered with lowered lances into a charge. Their heavily armoured destriers – the great war-horses that were led during the march and mounted only at the moment of battle – sprayed cumbrously through the impeding water towards the marshy bank. It was a battle against very heavy odds.

They had two things in their favour: cover from their bowmen, and the desperate knowledge that the chance of dying in the passage of the Somme was a better option than the certainty of death or disgrace if they remained on the south bank. 'And stoutly the knights fought; and both sides shot arrows and cast spears; but the men of Picardy were soon broken and put to flight, together with Sir Godemar, and with the help of God all passed in due time.'

The English vanguard spilled over the undulating fields of Ponthieu, through the town of Rue to Le Crotoy on the estuary. The middle ward and rearguard rattled and splashed across the river; only a few carts and stragglers fell into the hands of Philippe who arrived at Saigneville when the tide was already flowing too strongly for him to pass. He turned back towards Abbeville, where he remained all next day, collecting reinforcements for his already vast army.

Although Edward was safely beyond the Somme, and had avoided certain annihilation, he was not a great deal better off than he had been for most of his journey northward from Paris. He could not increase his speed of march without sacrificing the cartloads of booty, much of which belonged not to him but to his army; the rapid progress through hostile country had resulted in a shortage of food, and of shoes and leather to replace and repair them. Béthune, where he had last heard his Flemish allies lay, was five days away. He knew himself to be greatly outnumbered, but he determined to turn and fight. Though

The crossing of the Somme at Blanche-Taque. Edward III can be recognized on the left by his crown and quartered surcoat.

he did not know it, it was the only decision that could save him. On the same day that he had crossed the Somme – 24 August 1346 – the Flemings abandoned the siege of Béthune and withdrew across their frontier.

Edward recalled his skirmishers, regrouped his army, and set his columns moving north-east along the rough tracks and rides of the great forest of Crécy-en-Ponthieu. At the edge of the woodland, on a rolling hillside above the village of Crécy, he found a good defendable position. His army slept that night under the cover of the trees. Early next morning (26 August), with the Prince of Wales and other commanders, he heard mass, confessed and received communion; then he formed a wagon park for his carts and horses at the fringe of the forest and marshalled his men on the hillside that sloped gently down to the Vallée des Clercs, which ran from Wadicourt Bottoms to the river Maye.

For the best part of three centuries it had been usual in most of Christendom for battles to be won by heavy cavalry. Neither the Saxon footsoldiers nor the Saracen light horse had been able to withstand the impact of mounted men-at-arms on their heavily barded steeds. In barbarous countries such as Scotland, the Norman ruling classes had trained their expendable serfs to form supposedly impenetrable phalanxes of shields and spears, but Edward I had shown at Falkirk that these could be broken up by archers before sending in the decisive cavalry charge. His son had met an ignominious defeat at Bannockburn because he forgot this lesson. Edward III, who had inherited many of the qualities of his famous grandfather, adapted and improved on his tactic at Halidon Hill when he shattered a Scottish charge not with a counter-charge but with arrows.

The English nation that the first Edward Plantagenet had determined to synthesize from Norman conqueror and dispossessed Saxon had become a reality under his grandson. Schoolboys were being taught to translate their Latin exercises into English, not French; Chaucer was a boy, Gower, Langland and Wycliffe were young men; popular songs were already being recorded in English. Parliament had abolished the unequal penalties for Normans and Englishmen for committing similar crimes, and in a few years would establish English as the language of the law courts. Villein tenants were metamorphosing into freemen farmers; burgesses with Saxon names were being returned to Parliament to sit with Norman knights. And on the field of battle an entirely new figure was emerging to stand beside the famous heroes of chivalry – the stalwart, anonymous English bowman: resolute in adversity, disciplined in success, from the fourteenth century to the introduction of indiscriminate automatic fire in the twentieth, from longbow and Brown Bess to Lee-Enfield, his tradition endured.

Edward ordered that the battle should be fought on foot. To his son he gave the place of honour and greatest danger, commanding the vanguard on the right of the line with the experienced support of the Earls of Warwick and Oxford, Harcourt, Holland, Chandos, Audley and many others. The rearguard, under the Earls of Northampton and Arundel, 'were on a wing in good order, ready to comfort the Prince's battle, if need be'. Edward seems to have stationed himself with the middle ward slightly to the rear of these two. The composition of these three 'battles' was not necessarily the same as it had been when the expeditionary force landed in Normandy six weeks earlier. It was the duty of the marshals (Edward had appointed Warwick and Harcourt at the outset, with Arundel as constable in charge of discipline) to allot the various contingents to their stations in accordance with the king's general plan.

Of the prince's battle, Froissart states categorically but confusingly that 'the archers there stood in manner of a herse and the men of arms in the bottom of the battle'. A 'herse' means a 'harrow' – but what exactly this harrow formation looked like has been the subject of much argument. Of the two predominant schools, one maintains that the 'harrow' was formed by the archers standing in quincunx pattern, representing the trellised links of a harrow, each line staggered behind the one in front so that the men shot through the gaps; the other claims that the archers were posted in wedges, like the pointed prongs of a harrow, protruding from each wing, so that their crossfire drove the enemy cavalry on to the men-at-arms who formed the greater part of the line (there is evidence that Edward used some archers in a position of this kind at Halidon).

Neither explanation is satisfactory. In each instance the archers would eventually have been ridden down by the enemy cavalry. The second, and recently more popular, explanation

49

also pays no regard to the number of men-at-arms in relation to archers and pikemen. No matter how exaggerated the figures given by contemporary chroniclers may be, the proportions remain constant. Jean Le Bel says the prince had at Crécy '1,200 men at arms, 3,000 archers and 3,000 Welsh [footmen]'. Northampton's battle had '1,200 men-at-arms and 3,000 archers', with the number of pikemen unspecified, as they also are in the king's battle of '1,600 men-at-arms and 4,000 archers'. Froissart reduced this to 'eight hundred men of arms and two thousand archers, and a thousand of other with the Welshmen ...; about eight hundred men of arms and twelve hundred archers ...; seven hundred men of arms and two thousand archers'. The ratio is still approximately two men-at-arms to every five archers and, by implication, a further five pikemen. Le Bel explicitly states that at the outset of the campaign Edward had 4,000 men-at-arms, 10,000 archers and 10,000 footmen. Thus it is clear that, even apart from the tactical objections, the men-at-arms were not numerous enough to have made up the bulk of the line, with the archers bunched on the flanks.

A solution that fits the descriptions without military absurdity is that archers and pikemen were posted alternately in at least two ranks along the whole line. The pikemen knelt while the archers shot over their heads. When the enemy cavalry closed on the front line, the archers drew their swords or, more probably, helped the pikemen hold firm their lances against the massive impact of the armoured horses. The men-at-arms 'in the bottom of the battle', i.e. standing behind the front ranks, then joined in a mêlée with those enemy riders who broke through the hedge, most of them already thrown or hooked out of their saddles. The archers rose and resumed shooting against the next wave of horsemen. If extra companies of archers (similarly protected by pikemen) were stationed on the wings, they were probably there for the purpose of preventing a flanking movement by the enemy cavalry, who would not only have caught the dismounted men-at-arms at a disadvantage but would also have captured their horses and transport. When the men-at-arms advanced, the archers on the wings could move with them, giving diagonal cover, while those in the line paused to shoot over their heads.

Infantry weapons. *Top*  The short sword carried by archers ...

*Above*  The bardiche, for cutting and piercing ...

*Below*  The bill, for cutting, piercing and hooking horsemen out of their saddles.

None of this could be done with the precision of a modern army, since each 'battle' was made up of mixed forces raised by individual commanders and fighting under their separate banners. A few of them wore distinctive uniforms, such as the Prince of Wales's Welsh and Cheshire levies in woollen courtepy and chaperon (short coat and cap), green on the right side and white on the left, but most had only a badge on the collar or sleeve, if they had anything at all. These were the indentured men – volunteers. To fill the gaps, deepen his defences, strengthen his wedges of archers or lines of pikemen, the marshal could use the conscripts chosen by the commissioners of array. These, too, probably had various rudimentary uniforms, since each man was entitled to a free suit of clothing from the county where he was arrayed.

As soon as his marshals had made their dispositions 'the King leapt on a small palfrey, with a white rod in his hand ... He rode from rank to rank desiring every man to take heed that day to his right and honour. He spake it so sweetly and with so good countenance and merry cheer, that all such as were discomforted took courage in the seeing and hearing of him. And when he had thus visited all of his battles it was then nine of the day; then he caused every man to eat and drink a little.' For this they evidently broke ranks and may well have been served with some sort of hot meal from field kitchens in the wagon park. 'And afterward they ordered again their battles: then every man lay down on the earth and by him his sallet [helmet] and bow, to be the more fresher when their enemies should come.' Despite Edward's reassuring words, they cannot have rested with quiet minds, for the French army against which they were committed to battle outnumbered them two and possibly three times. (Le Bel, who gives Edward's army as 24,000, says that Philippe had '20,000 mounted men-at-arms and more than 100,000 men on foot'. The series of contemporary chronicles known as the *Brut* reports that the French king had '4 battles the least of which passed greatly the number of the English'. Froissart says that Edward 'had not the eighth part in number of men that the French King had'.)

It was not until well into the afternoon that the French columns were seen advancing from the direction of Marcheville, two or three miles away. Hastily assembled from different

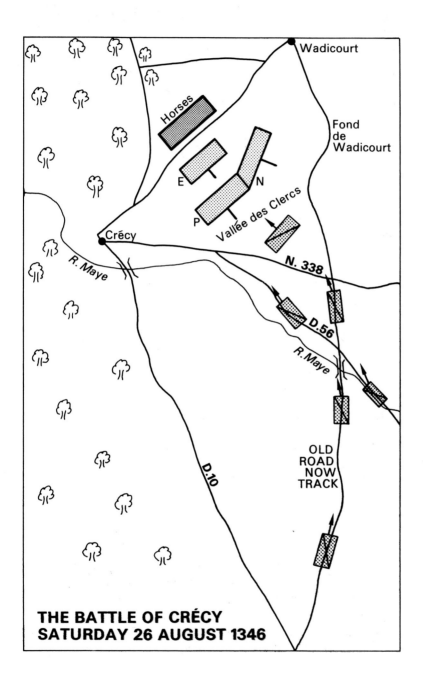

Wadicourt

Horses

Fond
de
Wadicourt

E          N

Vallée des Clercs

P

Crécy

R. Maye

N. 338

D.56

R. Maye

OLD
ROAD
NOW
TRACK

D.10

**THE BATTLE OF CRÉCY**
**SATURDAY 26 AUGUST 1346**

quarters, disordered by forced marching, inadequately marshalled, they advanced in mob order under a lowering sky.
Philippe sent instructions forward that the army was to encamp
for the night. His commanders, hot with pride and thirsty for
revenge (and perhaps suspecting that their king was once more
trying to avoid battle), refused to obey. 'None of these lords
was willing to turn back, if those in front of them would not
turn back first; and those who were in front would not turn
back because it seemed shameful to them ... So they rode on
through pride and envy, without order, the one before the other
... until they saw the English ranged in three battles facing
them right featously. And then it was still more shameful to
turn back when they saw their enemy so near.' A vast flock
of crows flew ominously across the valley, the black clouds
opened and 'there fell a great rain and a flash of lightning with
a terrible thunder'.

The 6,000 Genoese crossbowmen who were to open the
French attack, 'weary of going afoot that day six leagues', protested that: 'we be not well ordered to fight this day ... We
have more need of rest.' Philippe's brother, Charles Count of
Alençon, commanded them to go forward. As they reluctantly
did so 'the air began to wax clear, and the sun to shine fair
and bright, the which was right in the Frenchmen's eyes and
on the Englishmen's backs'. The Genoese formed into line,
encouraged themselves with a loud yell, and began to move
up the slope. They halted and shouted again. The English line
remained silent and motionless. The crossbowmen came within
their own effective range of two hundred yards. They halted
for the third time. Again they shouted. 'Then they shot fiercely
with their crossbows. Then the English archers stept forth one
pace and let fly their arrows so wholly together and so thick,
that it seemed snow.'

Each man carried a quiver of twenty-four arrows, with
another twenty-four set upright in a hole grubbed out at his
feet. Pages and pikemen stood ready to race forward with more
arrows from the supply carts. An English archer could loose
off from six to ten aimed arrows a minute, while the crossbowmen, who had to lower their bows and, with hands and
foot, strain and latch the spring after each shot, could manage
no more than two. 'When the Genoways felt the arrows piercing

A mail shirt of
1340.

through heads, arms and breasts, many of them cast down their crossbows and did cut their strings and returned discomfited.' Another account claims that they retreated because their bow-strings had been affected by the torrential rain (the English archers kept theirs dry by coiling them up and putting them under their helmets). And a third version says that 'the English fired three cannons, by which it happened that the Genoese crossbowmen who were in the front ranks turned their backs and ceased shooting'. If this is true, it was the first time that Edward had used cannons on the battlefield, though he seems to have experimented with them as siege weapons a dozen years before.

Whatever the reason for the Genoese mercenaries' defection – and sheer professional despair over an attack launched in such a haphazard manner may have had a good deal to do with it – their retreat turned out to be as hazardous as their advance. Philippe shouted: '"Slay those rascals, for they shall let and trouble us without reason!" Then ye should have seen the men of arms dash in among them and killed a great number of them: and ever still the Englishmen shot whereas they saw the thickest press; the sharp arrows ran into the men of arms and into their horses, and many fell, horse and men, among the Genoways, and when they were down they could not raise themselves again, the press was so thick that one overthrew another.'

A new line of French horsemen formed, surged forward, ploughed and stumbled through the remnants of the cross-bowmen and the first men-at-arms, and then faltered under the rain of arrows. So one wave after another broke as it came up the slope. The French nobility screamed defiance and reproach at the English who would not get on their horses and come out and fight in a chivalrous fashion. 'But the Englishmen never departed from their battles for chasing of any man, but kept still their field, and ever defended themselves against all such as came to assail them.'

And still the English bowmen 'shot so marvellously that, when the horses felt the barbed arrows ..., one would not go forward, another leaped uphill as if mad, another bucked hideously, another turned his croup to the enemy despite his master ...; and the English lords, being on foot, advanced and

The Battle of
Crécy. The Prince
of Wales stands
with his sword
raised (*centre left*)
and his standard
bearer, Richard
FitzSymon, beside
him.

struck at these men who could find no help in themselves or
in their horses'. But the French continued to press upon the
English vanguard and eventually by sheer weight of numbers
'perforce opened the archers of the Prince's battle and came
and fought with the men of arms hand to hand ... In this so
terrible a bickering the Prince of Wales, being then but sixteen
years old, showed his wonderfulle towardnesse, laying on very
hotly with speare and shielde ... Then the second battle of the
Englishmen came to succour the Prince's battle, the which was
time, for they had as then much ado.'

It seemed for a while that the intervention of Northampton's
division would not save the day. 'And the Prince of Wales was
so deep in the fray that twice he was brought to his knees and
his standard bearer, Sir Richard FitzSymon, took his banner
and put it beneath his feet and straddled it to guard it and to
help his master at the same time; and he took his sword in both

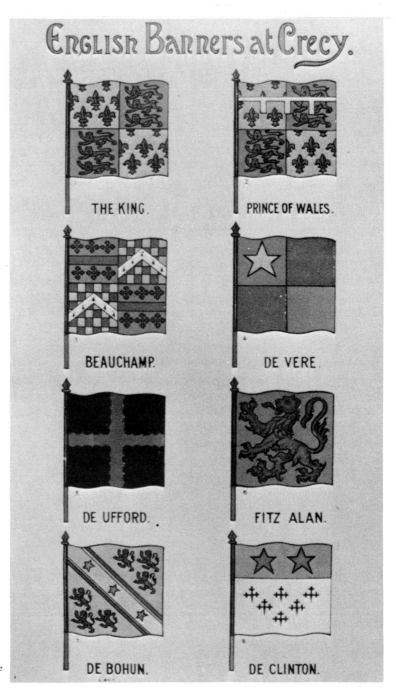

Banners used at the
Battle of Crécy.

hands and began to defend the Prince, shouting "Edward and St George! to the King's son!" At this the Bishop of Durham and many valiant knights went to the Prince's rescue, and then Sir Richard raised his banner again.' Warwick and Oxford sent an urgent message to the king, who was observing the course of the battle from a windmill on a ridge at the rear, just to the east of the Crécy–Wadicourt road (D.111): 'Such as be about the Prince your son, are fiercely fought withal and are sore handled; wherefore they desire you that you and your battle will come and aid them; for if the Frenchmen increase ... your son and they shall have much ado.'

Edward was unperturbed. He was also no doubt wary of exposing his right flank and rear to an attack up the road from Crécy if he moved forward. 'Return to him and to them that sent you hither,' he replied to the messenger, 'and say to them that they send no more to me for any adventure that falleth, as long as my son is alive; and also say to them that they suffer him this day to win his spurs; for if God be pleased, I desire this day to be his and the honour thereof, and to them that be about him.' The prince and his men beat off the attack, the line was re-formed, the din of battle continued. In wave after wave – more than a dozen massive attacks – the flower of French chivalry supported by Philippe's German allies flung themselves against the English line without success. Philippe, who rediscovered his courage once he was committed to action, had two horses killed under him and was wounded by arrows in the throat and thigh. His fifty-one-year-old brother-in-law, the King of Bohemia, almost totally blind but still eager to fight, ordered his companions to 'bring me so far forward that I may strike one stroke'. They led him into the thick of the fight, where he 'struck as many friends as foes, and more, with his sword', and in the morning they were all found dead together.

It was dusk before Philippe allowed himself to be persuaded to leave the field and avoid the increasing risk of capture. For his lack of control and their own proud insubordination his vassals and allies had paid a terrible price. Besides the King of Bohemia, the dead included the Duke of Lorraine and the Counts of Alençon, Auxerre, Flanders, Harcourt (the brother of Geoffroi), Salm, Sancerre and Vaudémont: a restrained assessment (some estimates give a total of more than 30,000) is: 'besides the Earls etc. mentioned above, 24 Bannerets, 1,200 knights, 1,500 Esquires, 4,000 archers on horseback, and commonalty, who were not counted.'

On the victorious slope the English 'made great fires and lighted up torches and candles', by whose light the king 'went with all his battle to his son the Prince and embraced him in his arms and kissed him, and said: "Fair son, God give you good perseverance; ye are my good son, thus ye have acquitted you nobly: ye are worthy to keep a realm." The Prince inclined himself to the earth, honouring the King his father.' There was no doubt that the praise was well deserved. Throughout the battle it was the prince's division that had borne the worst of the attack. Courage and obedience to his father's orders had earned him a major share of credit for the victory.

The next day was a Sunday. While a large body of horsemen scoured eastward in search of further Frenchmen, and three heralds searched the misty field to identify the illustrious dead, the king went to mass and made his plans for the future. There was no longer any breathless hurry to reach Béthune, and he had no doubt received news from Hugh Hastings by now that the Flemings had raised the siege three days before and retreated. During the course of the morning his heavy reconnaissance force came upon French levies from Rouen and Beauvais making their way towards the battle that they did not know was already lost. The unfortunate Frenchmen were taken by surprise and suffered heavy casualties. Edward, all opposition dispersed, suddenly saw the prospect of turning his defiant raid into a war of acquisition. Burning a broad path up through Montreuil and Hesdin to Wissant, he arrived outside Calais on 4 September. Here was a great prize, if he could take it. The haven from which French privateers preyed upon English shipping would be converted into a fortress gateway for excursions into France whenever it pleased him.

The military governor of Calais, a sturdy Burgundian named Jean de Vienne, refused Edward's demand that he surrender the town, counting on his high double walls and double ditch to protect him until Philippe could raise and bring to his rescue a new army. Edward, who had many men eager to return home with their spoils and was not strong enough in artillery to carry the fortifications by assault, settled down to impose a blockade.

A knight (Sir Geoffrey Luttrell) fully armoured and mounted on his war-horse. His wife and daughter-in-law are handing him his helmet and shield.

He sent orders to England for the immediate supply of 'Corn, wine, ale, meat, fish, bows, arrows and bowstrings', and set about providing his army with snug winter quarters behind a double moat which he dug along the marshes to the west of the town. On the sandy dunes between this moat and the sea his carpenters made 'houses and lodgings of great timber, and set the houses like streets and covered them with reed and broom, so that it was like a little town; and there was everything to sell, and a market place to be kept every Tuesday and Saturday for flesh and fish, mercery ware, houses for cloth, for bread, wine and all other things necessary, such as came out of England or out of Flanders'. Queen Philippa joined Edward there, while their eldest son returned to England where Parliament 'thanked God for the victory He had granted their liege lord ... and said that all the money they had given him at that time had been well spent'.

61

Chapter Three

# The King's Lieutenant

The diversionary operations that Henry of Lancaster had been sent to carry out in Gascony in 1345 had been very successful. In the summer and autumn of that year he gained spectacular victories over the French at Bergerac, Auberoche, La Réole and Aiguillon, and in 1346 he stormed Saint-Jean-d'Angély, Lusignan and Poitiers in turn. He was back in Bordeaux at the end of October, and in England by 1 January 1347. In London he paid a visit to a distinguished captive in the Tower – David, King of Scotland. When Edward invaded France, Philippe had urged David to launch an attack: 'The land of England is left without defence, for the greater part of his army is with him, and another part in Gascony, and another divided between Flanders and Brittany ... If you will act with speed and energy you can inflict great damage on him.' David crossed the border with a large army, but at Neville's Cross he was wounded in the head with an arrow and captured by the local levies whom Edward had wisely left at home.

There was victory on every hand – except at Calais, where Jean de Vienne still held out, waiting for the relieving columns. Early in the siege he had expelled a great number of old men, women and children – useless mouths that could not aid the defence but would consume valuable stores. Edward magnanimously 'suffered them to pass through his host without danger, and gave them meat and drink to dinner and every person twopence sterling in alms'. But when, a few months later, Vienne tried the same trick again, Edward drove them back into the city.

The moment of decision was approaching. Early in April 1347 a French fleet of thirty ships slipped past the English block-

Henry, Duke of Lancaster, one of the original members of Edward III's Order of the Garter (from the fifteenth-century Bruges Garter Book).

ade, but that was the last considerable supply of food that Vienne received. Time was running out for Edward too. Losses from dysentery and desertion began to outpace the reinforcements the Prince of Wales sent from England. Word came from inland that Philippe had summoned a new army larger even than the one that had been defeated at Crécy, to assemble at

Arras on 20 May 1347. But French organization and discipline was as lax as ever. Philippe advanced as far as Hesdin in the last fortnight of June and there settled down to await 'the commons' whose military skill he and his aristocracy so foolishly despised and neglected.

From beleaguered Calais fifty miles away Vienne continued to despatch secret messages imploring help. On 25 June a boat trying to sneak out of the harbour was driven ashore by the English patrol. Just before it grounded, its captain was seen to throw something overboard. At low tide the object was recovered and brought to Edward. It was an axe-head, to which was tied a letter from Vienne to his 'right dear and dreaded lord' assuring him that 'we are all well and of good courage and right willing to serve you, ... yet the town is in dire need of corn, wine, and meat. For there is nothing here that has not been eaten – dogs, cats and horses – we can find no more victuals in the town except we eat human flesh.'

It was more than three weeks before Philippe moved. Edward, having strengthened his vulnerable west flank (he was protected on the east and south by marshes impassable to cavalry), sent Henry of Lancaster out on a foraging raid that produced 2,000 cattle and 5,000 sheep. On Friday 27 July Philippe at last arrived on the tall dunes at Sangatte. He had marshes on his right, the sea with English vessels and English archers in their 'castles' on his left, and in front of him the river Hem, its only bridge held by Lancaster and the approaches covered by more archers in ships that had been run ashore on the sand. The roads through the marsh from the south had been cut with deep wide ditches. That night the Calais garrison lit fires, shouted, blew trumpets and banged drums. The next night the fire was smaller, the noise less. On the third night the light was scarcely visible, the defiant cries had dwindled to a low moan. The intended message was evidently that they could barely hold out any longer.

Philippe sent heralds to Edward demanding free passage to his town of Calais, or alternatively that Edward should come out and fight him. 'When King Edward heard these words he thought for a little, then said ...: "Tell him from me that I have been here nearly a year, within his sight and knowledge; he could have come earlier, if he had wanted, but he has let me remain here so long that I have spent much and I believe I have done enough to be shortly lord of the fair town of Calais. It is not my intention to do just as he wishes, for his convenience or his pleasure, nor to give up what I have won or believe I shall win. And if he cannot pass by one road, let him pass by another."'

To this sturdy commonsense reply, Philippe produced another of his empty romantic gestures: a challenge to Edward of 'hand-to-hand battle of a hundred against a hundred, a thousand against a thousand, or man against man'. Edward replied the next day – 1 August – that he accepted. It was a gamble – but he had got the measure of his opponent. During that night Philippe withdrew. The English cavalry attacked the French rearguard, capturing stores and tents. Philippe's great army dispersed in confusion while the Prince of Wales, back again from England, pursued with a raiding party that 'set fire and flame to all the country round' for a distance of seventy miles or more.

The unfortunate Jean de Vienne appeared on the walls, signalling that he wished to discuss terms. Edward at first insisted on unconditional surrender, but eventually agreed 'that they let six of the chief burgesses of the town come out bare-headed, bare-footed, and bare-legged, and in their shirts, with halters about their necks, with the keys of the town and the castle in their hands, and let them six yield themselves purely to my will, and the residue I will take to mercy'.

Six rich and brave burgesses volunteered to be the hostages. The ensuing scene – in which they begged for mercy and Edward ordered them to be beheaded but was finally persuaded to let them go free by the intercession of the ever-pregnant Queen Philippa – is famous through Froissart's account and Rodin's statue. The most remarkable feature of the incident – and the one that is always misrepresented – is not Edward's harshness but his leniency. For the conventions of war were quite clear on this point. At the beginning of a siege, the garrison commander and the townspeople were called upon to let the besieging troops enter. If they refused and the enemy was compelled to expend lives and material in forcing them to surrender, then their own lives and property were forfeit – they well knew that these were the stakes for which they

The mêlée at a tournament. The contestants, having charged one another with lances, resort to swords.

gambled. The penalty applied to the citizens as much as to the garrison, since the town could be surrendered independently of the fortress, and often was. (The accepted form of surrender was for the elders, bare-headed and bare-footed, to bring out the keys to the besieger – this procedure was in no way peculiar to Calais.) Lancaster had put the town of Poitiers to the sword less than a year before because the leading citizens had refused to surrender. He had conversely 'commanded that no man should do any hurt to the town of La Réole nor to none of them within' when the citizens – but not the garrison – surrendered to him in 1345.

The lily banner of France was lowered, the lions quartered with the lilies were raised. The townspeople were evicted. The king

had a proclamation made throughout his realm of England that all who wished to live in Calais would be provided with houses and guaranteed protection if they arrived by September. To his triumphant barons and knights he gave a splendid banquet, at which he was seen to pay a great deal of attention to the nineteen-year-old Countess of Salisbury – 'the most beautiful woman in the whole realm of England and the most tender'. This famous beauty was the king's cousin, Joan of Kent, who had been adopted by Queen Philippa and had grown up with the Prince of Wales. When she was twelve she was married to another playmate of exactly her own age: William Montagu. Recently, while Montagu had been sharing glory with the Prince of Wales in the Normandy campaign, his young wife had won similar fame by her defence of the castle of Wark (a property belonging to her mother) against the invading Scots.

Her arrival at Calais was greeted with great enthusiasm, notably from the king. 'Every man regarded her marvellously; the King himself could not withhold his regarding of her, for he thought that he never saw before so noble nor so fair a lady. He was stricken therewith to the heart, with a sparkle of fine love, that endured long after.' He chose her as his partner in the ball that followed the banquet. Whether as a result of the strenuous dancing, or of some incident before they took the floor, the young countess (her husband had succeeded to the Salisbury title when his father was killed in the Windsor tournament in 1344) was seen to lose her garter. Edward's enthusiastic interest in the opposite sex was well known at court – rumour said not only that he had made previous attempts on the countess's honour, but that her husband was one of his illegitimate children. He was not a man to be embarrassed by such a reputation, so it is impossible to be sure whether he was frowning or smiling as he picked up the piece of blue velvet, tied it around his own leg, and remarked to the company: '*Honi soit qui mal y pense!*' ('Shame upon him who thinks ill of it!') The dancing continued.

By 14 October, having signed a truce to last until the next summer, Edward was back in London, ordering tournaments in honour of the victorious campaign in France to be held at Bury St Edmunds, Eltham and Windsor. It was at these tournaments that the king, the Prince of Wales and some other favoured knights first appeared 'in gownes of russet, powdered with garters blue, wearing the like garters also on their right legs, and mantels of blue with scutcheons of St George' and the motto *Honi soit qui mal y pense!* Christmas 1347 was spent by the court in jollifications at Guildford. In January 1348, quite unremarked except by some local traders, three merchant galleys from the Levant arrived at Genoa; later they continued to Marseilles.

While the king confronted Parliament and successfully won from them agreement to a tax of one-fifteenth for the next three years in anticipation of a renewal of the war with France, the Prince of Wales set up his own household. The king no longer referred to himself as 'Governor and administrator of Edward our first born'. The boy had won his spurs and his independence. He seems never to have visited Wales, and Chester very infrequently, but he stayed often at his house in Fish Street in the City, at the palace on his manor of Kennington and, for preference, at Berkhamsted, where he indulged in his passion for hawking.

His household grew: knights, squires and valets, keepers of his armoury, his destriers, the swans on the Thames that his father gave him, his marshals and butlers, the dean and priests of his chapels, his barber and barge-master and a dozen barge-men, his tent-makers and the keeper of his cellars, the clerks of the kitchen and food stores, the heralds and valets of the chamber and messengers. And for their offices and depots and accommodation and his own, while the great palace at Kennington was being built and enlarged, he rented a house near Candlewick Street and later took over a former lord mayor's mansion, and the bishop's palace in Ely Place. He was allotted rooms in the Palace of Westminster, and even then sometimes found it convenient to lodge on the Abbot of Westminster's manor at Poplar.

Ladies of quality travelling by coach.

He was devout, lavish in his gifts to the Church. He was also a fierce young man, eager for more war and, if the truce made war impractical at the moment, then for the jousting that simulated war. To those who fought with and against him in the lists he gave expensive presents of horses and armour; to those who entertained him at other times he gave keepsakes of precious metal, such as the enamelled silver beaker to his 'cousin Jeanette' at Christmas 1348. Jeanette and he shared a love of costly clothes. It was a time when women were decked with velvets, silks and furs brought back as booty from France. 'There was no woman of any condition who had not her share of the spoils of Calais, Caen and other places across the sea: clothes, furs, cushions and household utensils, tablecloths and necklaces, gold and silver cups, linens, were to be found in houses throughout England. English ladies were to be seen going about proudly in the dresses of French women.'

Dresses were high-waisted, clinging to the figure, men's tabards were shortened into doublets, with hip belts, perhaps in imitation of the victorious soldiers' jupon and sword-belt. Shoes, which had been square for a while, were pointed and padded and grotesquely curved upward. Fashions were growing more colourful and extreme, though not yet with quite the abandon that prompted Chaucer's parson to denounce them for their 'superfluity in length, ... trailing in the dung and the mire', for the 'cost of embroidering the elaborate indentation or adorning with bars or wavy lines, stripes, twists and bends, and similar waste of cloth in vanity', for the 'costly furring of their gowns, so much punching with chisels to make holes, so much dagging with shears', and at the same time for 'the horrible disordinate scantness of clothing, as be these cut sloppes or hainselins [jackets], that through their shortness cover not the shameful members of man, to wicked intent. Alas, some of them show the protuberance of their shape, and the horrible swollen members, that seemeth lyk the maladie of hernia, in the wrapping of their hoses, and also the buttocks of them appear as it were the hinderpart of a she-ape in the full of the moon.'

'A yeoman arrays himself as a squire, a squire as a knight, a knight as a duke and a duke as a King,' complained the Commons, ordering that 'carters, ploughmen, oxherds, cowherds,

Gentleman being
helped to dress by
the bedroom fire.

shepherds, swineherds, dairywomen and other keepers of
beasts, threshers of corn and all manner of men engaged in hus-
bandry, and all other people who do not own goods and chattels
to the value of 40s, shall wear no cloth except blanket and russet, 12d the yard, and shall have girdles and linen according
to their condition.' 'It seemed to the English that a new sun
was rising, because of abounding peace, plentiful goods and
glorious victory.'

A harsh corrective was at hand. The vile disease that the
three Levantine galleys had brought westward through the
Mediterranean, far from its original breeding ground in central
China, made its way up through Italy and France. In the summer of 1348, shortly after the hastiludes to celebrate the birth
of Philippa's twelfth recorded child – the short-lived William
of Windsor (the second of that name) – 'the grievous pestilence
penetrated the seacoast by Southampton and came to Bristol,
and there almost the whole strength of the town died, struck
as it were by sudden death; for few kept their beds more than
three days, or two days, or even half a day; and afterwards this
cruel death broke forth on every side, following the course of
the sun'. The sickness came in two forms: accompanied by fever
and spitting of blood, or by fever and carbuncles. The first,
pneumonic plague, was the more infectious and almost always
fatal, its victims' bodies being marked with the small black pus-
tules which gave the disease its name. The second, bubonic
plague, was spread by fleas, and from this some victims recovered, though contemporaries claimed that 'all that ever

'Each had on his head a cap marked with a red cross in front and behind. Each had in his right hand a scourge with three tails, each of which had a knot (and through the middle of some of these sharp nails were fixed). They marched barefooted one behind the other ...' A procession of Flagellants, 1349.

were born after that pestilence had 2 teeth less in their head than they had before'.

The Black Death struck at young and old, rich and poor, righteous and unrighteous. 'Reaching London about the Feast of All Saints [1 November 1348], it slew many people daily and spread so widely that from the Feast of the Purification [2 February 1349] until just after Easter more than 200 persons were buried every day in a newly-made cemetery at Smithfield.' The Prince of Wales's sister Joanna, on her way to marry Don Pedro, the heir to the throne of Castile, succumbed to the disease soon after reaching Bordeaux. So many priests were stricken that the pope issued a general absolution, to last until the following Easter. In Germany the authorities organized a great public burning of Jews, whom they accused of spreading the plague. There were other specifics. 'About Michaelmas 1349 more than six hundred men came to London from Flanders, mostly natives of Zeeland and Holland. Sometimes at St Paul's and sometimes at other points in the city they appeared twice a day clothed from the thighs to the ankles, but otherwise stripped bare. Each had on his head a cap marked with a red cross in front and behind. Each had in his right hand a scourge with three tails, each of which had a knot (and through the middle of some of these sharp nails were fixed). They marched barefooted one behind the other and whipped themselves with these scourges on their naked bleeding bodies. Four of them chanted in their own tongue and another four chanted in response ... Thus proceeding they would all cast

Cockfighting – a popular spectator sport among both rich and poor.

themselves on the ground, stretching out their hands in the shape of a cross. The singing went on and, the one who was in the rear acting first, each in turn stepped over the others and gave one stroke with his scourge to the man lying under him. This went on from the first to the last until all of those on the ground had observed the same ritual. Then each put on his customary garments and, still with their caps on their heads and their whips in their hands, they returned to their lodgings. It is said that they performed the same penance every night.'

At some time during this dreadful period of the plague – probably on St George's Day, 1348 – the king held the first official tournament at Windsor of the Order of the Garter that he had founded in honour of the Lady Joan. But the lady who inspired all this saw nothing of the celebrations. Soon after the fall of Calais, Sir Thomas Holland had gone to Rome to ask for the annulment of Joan's marriage to Salisbury – on the grounds that when she married Salisbury in 1341 she was in fact already Holland's wife, they having in the previous year declared themselves husband and wife in front of witnesses and subsequently lived together. Joan supported Holland's plea, whereupon Salisbury shut her up, a prisoner in her own home. It was not until November 1349 that the pope gave his decision – to quash the Salisbury marriage and restore Joan to Holland.

Cooks at work on stews and roasts, pounding, stirring, basting and turning the spit.

At Christmas 1349 the king discovered that one of the senior officers at Calais, Aimeri of Pavia, had been offered 20,000 gold crowns to surrender the fortress to Geoffroi de Charney, commander of the French garrison at Saint-Omer. Aimeri, who possibly revealed the plot voluntarily, was brought to Westminster for questioning. Edward then ordered him to proceed with the proposed betrayal and to tell Charney's agents that the castle would be handed over to them at midnight on 31 December. During the night of 30 December, Edward sailed into the port at Calais with the Prince of Wales and a strong company of men-at-arms. They entered the castle secretly and remained hidden throughout the following day.

After dark on the 31st Charney approached the town and sent two messengers to confirm that Aimeri was prepared to keep his promise. Aimeri assured them that he was. Charney then moved up his troops across the Nieulay bridge over the river Hem, sent a detachment with the 20,000 crowns to pay Aimeri and take over the fortress, and himself led the remainder to the Boulogne Gate, through which he was to enter the town.

As soon as Aimeri had received his bribe, Edward and his men attacked the Frenchmen, forced them to surrender, and locked them in a tower. The king then leaped on his horse and galloped to the Boulogne Gate. He ranged his men just inside, supported by a company of archers. The gate opened – and Charney suddenly found himself and his men assailed by a storm of arrows, followed by a line of charging cavalrymen, led by the king, 'raging like a Wild Boar, and crying out for in-

dignation as his usual manner was, "Ha! St Edward! Ha! St George!"'

The French quickly recovered their wits and began to fight back. Edward, lost in the rare enjoyment of hand-to-hand fighting to the death, allowed himself to be cut off on a causeway and for a time it looked as though he might be taken prisoner or killed. But the Prince of Wales saw the danger and hacked his way through to his father's side. The rest of the garrison, whom Edward had not alerted for fear that his trap would be revealed, came hurrying out of the fortress and the town. The French withdrew, leaving many dead or prisoners.

Before leaving Calais Edward gave Charney and the captured French knights a banquet at which he and they were served at their first course by the Prince of Wales and others of the victors. When all had finished their meal, Edward walked over to Eustace de Ribemont, with whom he had fought desperately at one period of the battle. 'Sir Eustace,' he said, 'I never found knight that gave me so much ado, body to body, as ye have done this day.' He took off a chaplet of gold and pearls (probably a richly decorated cap) that he was wearing and placed it on Ribemont's head: 'I desire you to bear it this year for love of me ... and I quit you of your prison and ransom.'

The rest of his prisoners were not as fortunate: he took them back to England to await their ransom. On his arrival the queen and all her ladies 'made great joy. Then said the King to his wife: "Lady dear, be pleased to entertain your son, for I should have been taken had it not been for his great valour, but by

75

The Great Seal,
showing the king
enthroned, used by
Edward III in
1348.

him was I succoured." "Sire," said she, "welcome be he and
you also. It seems that I should say: 'In a good hour was he
born.'"'

Aimeri was allowed to keep his bribe from Charney as a reward for his double dealing, but he did not live long to enjoy
it. Shortly afterwards he was captured by Arnoul d'Audrehem,
Marshal of France, who declared him guilty of treason and con-

demned him to have his flesh torn away with pincers, the tendons of his heels cut, his tongue wrenched out, and then to be hanged and quartered.

Despite the strenuous efforts of the pope, anxious to make a success of the approaching Jubilee Year, neither side was willing to enter into serious peace talks. France had concluded a naval treaty with Castile, and in the late autumn of 1349 a fleet of great Spanish galleys passed up the Channel, carrying merchandise to Flanders and attacking English shipping as it went. Edward determined to strike at it as it returned. He had plenty of time to plan the operation, for no admiral would willingly expose his ships during winter. In fact it was well into the summer of 1350 before he received warning that the Spaniards were about to leave Sluys, having taken on extra men and munitions – for they in turn were aware that Edward had ordered ships and seamen to be impressed in July to join the fleet that he had begun equipping two months earlier. On 10 August Edward asked the Archbishops of Canterbury and York to have prayers offered for victory in his forthcoming engagement. A few days later he set off with the Prince of Wales and a great band of noble warriors to Winchester and then Southampton. There they went aboard their ships and sailed eastward to confront the Spaniards as they came through the Straits of Dover. The king, who never missed an opportunity to raise his troops' morale before battle, put on a black velvet jacket and a black beaver hat, and posted himself conspicuously on the forecastle of his ship. He called upon his military band – five trumpeters, one citoler (who played a sort of guitar), five pipers, two drummers (one on the tabor, the other on the naker), two clarioners, one fiddler and three waits (who played the shawm) – to make music while Sir John Chandos sang the words of a new dance tune that he had brought back from Germany, where he had been on crusade against the heathen Prussians.

They were off Winchelsea when the man on watch suddenly called, '"Ho! I see one coming and it looks like a ship of Spain." Then the minstrels ceased and he was asked if he saw more.

'It seems that I should say: "In a good hour was he born."' Queen Philippa, sketched from a mural formerly in St Stephens Chapel, Westminster.

Edward Prince of
Wales, as sketched
from the same
mural.

Quite soon after he answered and said, "Yes I see two – and three – and four." And then, when he saw the main fleet, "I see so many, God help me, that I cannot count them." ... Then the King had his trumpets sound, and all their ships drew together and set themselves in order.'

The English ships, ranging from small barges to the great vessels of the Bordeaux wine trade with crews of fifty men or more, were laden with archers, men-at-arms, stones for throwing and castles to throw them from. These wooden castles, built both fore and aft, had been in use for at least a century. In early times they were installed by carpenters each time a ship was commandeered for military purposes. Recently many new ships had been provided with castles at the time they were built, to defend them from pirates and freebooters. Since the ships were not big enough to carry more than the most rudimentary artillery, the only way they could deal with an enemy ship was either to ram it or to board it. The size of the Spanish vessels, longer, broader and taller than most of the English ('like as Castles to Cottages') usually precluded the first possibility. Edward's seamen had to lay their ships alongside so that the men-at-arms could scramble aboard and fight it out toe to toe. This they did under cover from the archers who, when the ships had grappled, set aside their bows and leaned out of the castles to throw down stones and quicklime on their opponents' heads, soft soap and caltrops beneath their feet.

The king ordered the captain of his own great ship to steer directly at the first Spanish vessel. They collided like a roll of thunder, the Spaniards' forecastle toppling over and throwing its occupants into the sea. The king's ship rebounded and he directed it against the next Spanish galley. This he boarded and captured, driving the defenders overboard.

'The young Prince of Wales and those of his ship were fighting in another part. Their vessel was grappled and held by a great Spanish ship. And there the Prince and his men had much to suffer, for their ship was split and holed in many places, so that water entered at great speed and it was only by much bailing that it was prevented from sinking immediately. Therefore the Prince's men fought right bitterly to overcome the Spanish ship; but they could not succeed, for it was stoutly defended.' Henry of Lancaster, bringing his ship alongside the prince's,

Jean II of France, called John the Good.

realized the danger that the king's son was in, 'for water was being thrown out in all directions'. He veered off, worked round to the other side of the Spaniard, and grappled with it. 'Then the Spaniards did not hold out long. Their vessel was conquered and they were all put overboard, without quarter. The Prince of Wales and his men took possession; scarcely had they done so when their own ship sank. Thus they could see most clearly the great peril they had been in.'

Exactly a week before the battle, on Sunday 22 August 1350, Philippe VI died and was succeeded by his eldest son. In response to further pleas from the pope, Edward reopened peace talks with the new king, but in such terms – he insisted on referring to him as 'Jean, son of Philippe de Valois' and repeating his claim to the throne of France – that he evidently saw no chance of agreement. His problems were in fact more domestic than foreign at this moment. The Black Death had left a legacy of unrest. In 1351 the mayor found himself compelled to warn the 'common lewd women who dwell in the City of London, and from other foreign parts resort unto the same city', who 'have now of late ... assumed the fashion of being clad and attired in the manner and dress of good and noble dames and

81

damsels', that they should not dare thenceforward to wear any clothes trimmed with miniver (the contrasting blue-grey back and white belly fur of a species of squirrel), badger fur, popelle or 'stranlyng' (fur of squirrels killed in spring and autumn), 'rabbit or hare or any other manner of noble budge', nor lined with sendal, buckram or silk – 'so all folks, natives and strangers, may have knowledge of what rank they are'.

This extravagant behaviour by the common people of the city reflected a general affluence produced by a shortage of labour. The plague had carried away so many – probably four people in every ten – that those who survived could demand higher wages and refuse to return to their former conditions. Landowners found their revenues painfully reduced. The dead could pay no rent; their heirs, instead of leaping joyfully into the vacant tenancies, demanded better terms. Parliament gave its approval in June 1349 to a Statute of Labourers which forbade employers to offer higher wages than had on average been paid during the five or six years before the plague. Men who refused to work for these wages were to be put in gaol. The result was not a stabilization of wages and prices but a general evasion of the law by all classes in their own interests.

The Prince of Wales, as one of the greatest landowners, had his share of these troubles. His property, in addition to the great estates of Wales, Chester and Cornwall, included many manors scattered throughout the south and midlands, in the counties of Somerset, Dorset, Gloucestershire, Worcestershire, Shropshire, Staffordshire, Warwickshire, Leicestershire, Rutland, Lincolnshire, Nottinghamshire, Derbyshire, Oxfordshire, Northamptonshire, Bedfordshire, Hertfordshire, Essex, Cambridgeshire, Huntingdonshire, Norfolk, Suffolk, Berkshire, Wiltshire, Hampshire, Surrey, Sussex, Buckinghamshire and Middlesex, yet most of them so small that the annual income from all (as recorded twenty years later) amounted to only £300, compared with £1,300 from Chester, £1,700 from South Wales, £2,350 from Cornwall and £3,000 from North Wales.

Revenues from his Welsh coal and lead mines dropped by ninety-five per cent; his tolls on boats and fishing dried up entirely for a time. Bad weather compounded the tensions left by disease. A bitter frost that lasted from early December 1352 to the middle of March 1353 was ended by a violent hurricane

Work in the fields – the peasants prune their trees in March.

Etienne Aubert
who, as Innocent
VI, reigned as
Pope from 1352 to
1362.

and immediately followed by 'so great a drought that from the month of March until the month of July there fell no rain into the earth, wherefore all fruits, seeds and herbs for the most part were lost'. The price of grain and vegetables soared. There had been minor troubles on the prince's estates in Buckinghamshire in the previous year; now there was open revolt against his agents in Cheshire and he was obliged to take a large armed company to support and protect the judges sent to deal with the ringleaders.

The truce that had nominally existed between France and England since 1347, though constantly broken on both sides, was renewed in 1353 and again in 1354. In April that year Edward offered to renounce his claim to the throne of France if Jean would in turn recognize Edward's independent sovereignty over Aquitaine, Anjou, Touraine, Maine, and the northern territory of Ponthieu with Calais and Guines. Jean, perhaps because he was perturbed by the alliance that he rightly suspected Edward was negotiating with his son-in-law, Carlos II, the King of Navarre, who also held large estates in Normandy, agreed to a provisional peace treaty on these lines, the minor details to be adjudicated by the pope, in whose presence it would be ratified in the autumn. In August the Prince of Wales went on a tour of inspection of his estates in Cornwall. By the time he returned it was beginning to be clear that Jean had changed his mind. Before Pope Innocent VI at Avignon the French ambassadors insisted that Edward must do homage for Gascony, the southernmost part of Aquitaine – thus destroying all hope of negotiation. Edward once more prepared for war.

On 7 January 1355 Philippa bore her eighth son and thirteenth recorded child, Thomas of Woodstock. For the celebratory tournaments that followed the baptism and his mother's churching in March, the Black Prince gave expensive presents of breastplates covered in black and red velvet to his friends, including Sir John Chandos and Sir James Audley, brothers-in-law who had fought by his side with his household chamberlain, Sir Nigel Loring, at Crécy and in the sea-battle off Winchelsea, and were to see much service with him in the future. Among many knights who came from abroad to these tournaments was Jean de Grailly, Captal de Buch, a notable Gascon warrior and founder member of the Garter, who acted as spokesman for several of his compatriots claiming the king's protection and retaliation against the King of France's lieutenant, Jean Count of Armagnac. The Prince of Wales was immediately enthusiastic at the prospect of action. It was he who broached the subject to the king. 'Sire,' he said to Edward, 'you know well that ... in Gascony the noble valiant knights love you so much that they suffer great hardship for your war and to gain you honour, and yet they have no leader of your blood. Therefore if you were of a mind to send one of your sons they would be the bolder.'

The thought was evidently already in the king's mind. The Gascons – the name was often loosely used to describe the inhabitants of the whole of Aquitaine, the south-west corner of France below the Loire, though Gascony was strictly only the district between the Garonne and the Pyrenees over which the Spanish Vascones had poured eight centuries before – were not French by descent nor in their customs. For more than two hundred years – since their duchess, Eleanor, married Henry II in 1152 – they had been subjects of the English crown, though

85

Comment le duc de lancastre et le duc de
bretne vindrent a paris pour eulz combat-
tenans le Roy. mais le roy prist le sauf-

N l'an. mil en ce mes-
mes ceus cinqte deux
la veille de la mie daust
en aoust se combati
mon seigneur Guy de
Neelle Seigneur d'au-
fremont lors mareschal de france en bretaigne. et fu le dit mareschal occis en la

dicte bataille. le Sire de Buquelet. le chal-
tellain de Beauuais et pluseurs autres nobles tant dudit pays de bretaigne come
dautres marches du royaume de france.

Item en icelui an. cccliij. le mardy
quart iour de decembre se dot combatre a
paris un duc dalemaigne appelle le duc de
breslue contre le duc de lancastre pur pa-
roles que le dit duc de lancastre deuoit a-
uoir dites du dit duc de breslue. dont il lap-
pella en la court du roy de france. Et un

the English king, as their duke, did homage for them to the King of France. Their merchants had stronger economic ties, notably the wine trade, with England than with France; their lords and lordlings, whose small estates peppered the country-side with fortresses, though responsible to an English seneschal and constable, enjoyed more liberty than they could expect under direct rule by the French king. But constant encroachment by France had produced a natural fear that one day they might find themselves without protection from across the sea. A visit from a member of the royal family – especially from the king's eldest son – would do much to dispel this danger-ous idea. And a vigorous renewal of the war would stimulate trade in the principal towns of Bordeaux, Dax and Bayonne, while providing the Gascon nobles with employment and the chance of profit.

In March the royal council at Westminster instructed the Prince of Wales to proceed to Gascony with an army and Edward informed the pope that because of French aggression he would not renew the truce when it expired in the summer. In accordance with his usual strategy, he ordered the Prince of Wales's attack in Gascony to be paralleled by the landing in Normandy of an army under Lancaster (whom he had raised from earl to duke in 1351) to link with an uprising led by Carlos of Navarre. At the same time he began preparations to lead an army of his own to Calais. It is clear that even if he could have collected sufficient men (he already had an army under the Earl of Northampton in Brittany as well as the garrison at Calais) he would not have found sufficient ships to transport them simultaneously. But the mere announcement of his plans, which he made as public as possible, calling upon the clergy to offer prayers for success, served to bewilder and inhibit Jean. On 10 July 1355 the Prince of Wales was appointed the king's lieutenant in Gascony; two days later, after making offerings at several shrines, he set out for Plymouth where all his forces were to assemble.

His own contingent, in addition to his domestic and secre-tarial household, was composed of 433 men-at-arms, 400 archers on horses, and 300 on foot. Among his principal sub-commanders were the Earls of Oxford, Salisbury, Suffolk and Warwick who, with Sir John de Lisle and Sir Reginald Cob-

*Opposite* January 1352. The inaugural banquet of the Order of the Star – the Knights of Our Lady of the Noble House of Saint-Ouen. Founded by King Jean in imitation of Edward's Order of the Garter, it began with 100 members and was intended to expand to 500, but it failed to survive the death or capture of many of the knights at Poitiers.

Edward Prince of Wales, a portrait taken from the fifteenth-century Bruges Garter Book.

ham, had raised a total of some 1,500 men. Their wages were 6s 8d a day for an Earl, 4s a banneret, 2s a knight, 1s an esquire or man-at-arms, 6d a mounted archer, 3d a foot archer, 2d a pikeman. The composition of the entire expeditionary force – probably 1,000 men-at-arms, 1,000 mounted archers, and only 500 infantry – gave a clue to its purpose. This was not an army seeking a pitched battle but a mobile raiding column.

Departure was delayed by bad weather and by a lack of ships, which had to be 'arrested' by the king's officers – there was one Admiral for the coast north of the Thames estuary, another for the coast south and west of it – provided with crews (at an unskilled rate of 3d a day), furnished with gangways (up to 30 feet by 5 feet) and partitioning hurdles (7 feet by 4 feet) if they were to transport horses, and marshalled at Plymouth and Southampton. They ranged in size from 30 tons to more than 200, awkward vessels with single square sails and crews varying from 14 to 160 men. On 9 September 1355 the twenty-five-year-old prince led this fleet south in the *Christopher*. By 20 September he was at Bordeaux.

The prince lodged himself in the archbishop's palace and, on the day following his arrival, went to the adjoining Cathedral of Saint-André to hear the formal proclamation of his appointment, to swear to observe the rights and customs of Gascony and to receive the oaths of loyalty of the civic officials and the great lords of the province. These brought him men as a practical proof of their allegiance – together with their knowledge (priceless in an age when maps were few and rudimentary) of routes, fords, fortresses, towns and boundaries. With his plans made and his horses rested after the debilitating voyage, the prince set out on Monday 5 October 1355 to make a massive *chevauchée* into the land of the French king's lieutenant Jean d'Armagnac, whose county had formerly been part of Aquitaine.

The word *chevauchée*, which simply means a ride on horseback, had a sinister ring to medieval ears. It meant fire, slaughter and devastation of towns, villages and great tracts of land whose inhabitants' only crime was to have the wrong man as their overlord. It was a means of denying that overlord the stores and wealth with which to make war; it was a means of humiliating him, of showing his vassals that he was incapable of shielding them. It was an operation that combined elements of economic, psychological and propaganda warfare with the simple brutalities of the protection racket. Since the fourteenth century was not intrinsically different from our own, it was the poor and the defenceless who suffered most. The overlord lost face, the underlings lost food, shelter, small savings, obscure virginities, limbs and life itself.

89

Edward of Woodstock has been accused of inhuman cruelty and ruthlessness because of the raid he led from the Atlantic to the Mediterranean at the end of 1355 and because of incidents at various sieges and battles afterwards. Some French historians have even suggested that it was these incidents which won him the nickname of the Black Prince. The charge is completely unwarranted. The prince followed an established and accepted practice. It was what the Scots did continually in northern England, what his father did in 1346 in Normandy, what the French themselves did frequently in Gascony and in their raids on the English coasts. That the prince perhaps did it more thoroughly and effectively is beside the point. In his own eyes and those of his contemporaries, all of whom observed a common code of chivalry, there was nothing disgraceful in his conduct.

The great punitive column set out with a train of sumpter horses and carts carrying stores – during the first week's march through friendly territory, the army would have to live on what it brought or could buy. They made their way through forests of tall narrow trees, and out onto an arid land of heather and gorse and the broom that had given the prince's forebears their nickname of Plantagenet. At Arouille, overlooking a steep valley on the edge of the Count of Armagnac's domains, the prince marshalled his force into the customary three divisions: the vanguard under Warwick and Cobham; the middleguard with the prince himself, Oxford and many commanders of lesser contingents, including the Captal de Buch; the rearguard under Salisbury and Suffolk. They retook Arouille, which had fallen into Armagnac's hands; then they plunged into enemy territory – fertile upland and rich valleys beside the rivers that brought water down from the Pyrenees to feed the Adour and the Garonne. They captured Monclar, where the prince chose to spend the night under the comfort of a roof but had to leap hurriedly from his bed when some unknown aggrieved citizen set fire to the place. Thereafter he made do with his great tent, though the weather – because of the two months' delay in setting out from England – was showing signs of becoming inclement. On Friday 16 October they marched up the broad rich valley of the Midour to Nogaro. Next day the Captal de Buch took the fortress of Plaisance on the Arros, the citizens having

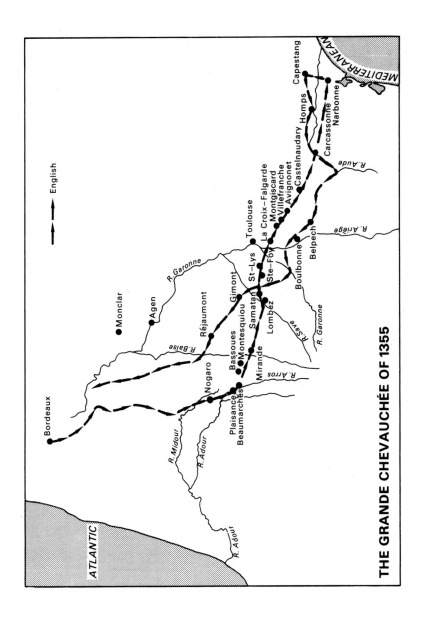

THE GRANDE CHEVAUCHÉE OF 1355

already fled from the town. They stayed two nights at Plaisance and burned it when they left on Monday. All this time skirmishers were stripping the surrounding villages and fields, bringing back food and fodder, jewels and money, and destroying all that they did not choose to carry. The road rose steeply from Beaumarchés to Bassoues, winding along a high ridge with views for miles on either side of horsemen scouring the cultivated lands and settlements. Bassoues was the Archbishop of Auch's land, and the prince, from policy as well as piety, had ordered that church property was to be spared. He would, in any case, have been hard put to it to reduce the great donjon that the archbishop had set up to dominate the valley, without the expense of too much time and too many lives. For the same reason he avoided Montesquiou, perched on its steep hill, and Mirande on the Baïse where the fortress looked strong and the garrison full of spirit. He was moving steadily eastward at a rate of seven or eight miles a day. The line of march was from one valley to the next over steep-domed hills, with the snow-tipped Pyrenees visible to the south after they left Mirande, making for Lombez. By now they had, as the prince wrote to the Bishop of Winchester, ridden right across 'the land of Armagnac, harrying and wasting the country, whereby the lieges of our most honoured lord [the king], whom the count had before oppressed, were much comforted'. But they had not encountered Armagnac himself. He had, in fact, been at Agen when the prince left Bordeaux and had followed a roughly parallel course to Toulouse, keeping the Garonne between himself and the invader and making no attempt to intercept. It appeared that he intended to establish himself and his larger army at Toulouse, thus preventing the English from advancing any further into Languedoc and, after allowing them to tire themselves with a siege if they wished, meet them in a pitched battle.

The prince continued up the wide valley of the Save, skirting Lombez, sacking and burning Samatan – 'as great a town as Norwich' – up a side valley and over a col to Sainte-Foy and thence out onto the wide plain to Saint-Lys. It was 26 October. Six hundred miles away Edward had that day landed at Calais to begin a similar *chevauchée* along France's northern territories. The prince halted for the whole of one day while scouts went out in search of information. They returned with confirmation that the count, still sheltering behind the walls of Toulouse, 'had broken all the bridges on both sides of the city, except those within it'. The prince took an astonishingly bold decision – to go straight ahead, across the uncrossable river, leaving an enemy army that greatly outnumbered his own on his flank.

It was a good day's march to reach the banks of the Garonne. 'There was no man in our host that knew the ford there but, by the grace of God, we found it,' wrote Sir John Wingfield. Men, horses and laden baggage wagons stumbled and lurched through the 'rough, rocky and marvellously terrifying' river and almost immediately afterwards through the Ariège, 'still more dangerous than the Garonne', for the prince had chosen to cross them one by one rather than face the added depth and breadth of the waters below their junction six or seven miles south of the city. 'They are very stiff and strong to pass,' he wrote to England. He lost some men and materials; but the gains were immense. By this astounding and contemptuous gesture he had made the Count of Armagnac look a fool and a coward.

From La Croix-Falgarde on the east bank of the Ariège he sent contingents north to fire villages and estates within sight of Toulouse, then continued through the 'very rich and plenteous' broad valley along what is now Route Nationale N.113, the Pyrenees still on his right, granite mountains on his left. Montgiscard, Villefranche, Avignonet, Castelnaudary: some were taken by storm; others surrendered and the citizens bought their lives with cash and valuables; all were stripped and burned. But now the dark line of the mountains that marched menacingly on the left began to draw in towards the foothills of the Pyrenees, forming a funnel that might well become a trap.

At the tip of the funnel, guarding the crossing of the Aude and the way out to the Mediterranean, stood the fortress town of Carcassonne, 'which is larger, stronger and more handsome than York'. In the six days since he had passed by Toulouse, panic had run before the prince, sweeping up those countryfolk who had means of transport, piling them into the bourg of Carcassonne on the left bank of the Aude. As his army approached, many of these, with the richer Carcassonnais, crossed the bridges and took refuge in the double-walled citadel, but enough stalwarts remained to force the vanguard to a smart skirmish, stubbornly defending their chain barriers street by street until they too were pushed back over the bridges. The citadel, perched 150 feet above the right bank of the Aude, was too strong to be stormed and could, even with its newly swollen population, have stood siege for weeks and even months. Once more, the prince had neither the time nor the men. He was, however, offered the opportunity to amass a great deal of money. A herald carrying a flag of truce came down the hill, bringing a proposal from the burgesses to pay a ransom of 250,000 gold crowns if the prince would spare the town from looting and fire. He replied that 'he had not come for gold but for justice' and that since they had refused to recognize his father as King of France, they were rebels unworthy of clemency or pardon.

The troops were given two days to rest and search for spoils while the prince and his council considered their next move. Narbonne and the Mediterranean lay only thirty-five miles away. To march with flame and sword from sea to sea would be a dazzling demonstration of Edward's power and Jean's futility. The problem was how to pass in comparative safety below the walls of the citadel: beneath a hail of stones and crossbow bolts. Having taken the decision to advance, the prince probably put a great deal of his wheeled transport across the bridge to the south bank by night. The remainder was given cover by archers, while most of the army followed the left bank until it found a spot where the river, abnormally low because of the parched summer following a dry spring, could be forded. Before they left, on Friday 6 November, they ensured that the town was well alight at several points. That same day, Thomas Stewart, Earl of Angus, led a Scottish seaborne raiding party into the Tweed and ransacked Berwick – a reprisal for which Jean of France had contributed men and money several months before.

Beyond Carcassonne the prince made good speed eastward. His vanguard was at Narbonne, 'a town but little smaller than London', by Sunday the 8th; and here, as at Carcassonne, the citadel on one side of the river was too strong to storm and well enough equipped with stone-throwing ballistae to make a stay in the town dangerous and unprofitable. It was, in any event, time to turn back. Winter was approaching; so too, at last, were the French. Jacques de Bourbon, Constable of France, was marching an army down from Limoges; Jean d'Armagnac had left Toulouse and was advancing east; a force of militia was said to be coming round the coast from Montpellier. From Avignon the pope sent two bishops with a plea that the prince should enter into peace talks with Jean, but the prince replied that Jean must talk with his father, of whose arrival in Calais he had just received news. He marched north to the sizeable town of Capestang, partly perhaps with the idea of dealing with the Montpellier militia before it could link with the other French armies, certainly partly because he did not intend to return by his outward route but to sear a second swathe of ruin across the rich countryside of Languedoc.

At Capestang he received more news: Jean d'Armagnac's army was only one or two days' march away. He regrouped to face this threat. The prime objective of the expedition, now that it was going home, was to preserve its booty. Already over-confidence, when they left Narbonne, had led to some of the carts being captured or destroyed in a sortie by the garrison. Swinging west the prince's vanguard entered Homps on Thursday 12 November and discovered that some of Armagnac's troops had been in the town the previous night but had now mysteriously disappeared. The prince marched on, apparently seeking out his enemy, but Armagnac had the heels of him. The French troops had been resting in Toulouse, while the English had covered more than three hundred miles, of which the last two days had been particularly rough, on stony roads with such a shortage of water that some of the horses had been given wine to drink. It was difficult to trace Armagnac's route in this alien territory. The prince continued west, split his forces in two and quested south beyond Carcassonne, then re-formed them again at Belpech to march peaceably through the lands of the Count of Foix, a known enemy of Armagnac and an influential leader whom it would be a great triumph to win over from allegiance to the King of France. The count, a cousin of the Captal de Buch, received the prince at the abbey of Boulbonne and feasted him before he continued his way across the Ariège.

The English army was some twenty miles south of Toulouse.

95

The prince would have chosen to pass on this side whether he was looking for Armagnac or not, for to go north of Toulouse would have meant exposing himself to attack from unknown numbers of French on his right while hemmed in by the Garonne on his left. But he still intended that his return journey should inflict as much damage as his outward one. After crossing the Garonne in a westward direction he therefore marched roughly north-west for twenty miles, intersecting his outward track before swinging left to continue parallel with it. By now Jean d'Armagnac had emerged from Toulouse once more. Reinforced by the armies of Jacques de Bourbon and Jean de Clermont, Marshal of France, who was the king's lieutenant in the territory above Languedoc between the Dordogne and the Loire, Armagnac now had so many men that they advanced in five divisions instead of the usual three. But he still seemed reluctant to press home a large scale attack or venture on a pitched battle.

On Friday 20 November, as he wheeled north-west after crossing the Garonne, the prince sent out a probing company of eighty lances under Audley and Chandos, who contacted a large group of Frenchmen, captured thirty of their knights and dispersed the remainder. Despite the disparity in numbers it seemed as if the English were on the attack still and the French defending. On Sunday the prince's vanguard came upon a new French concentration blocking their path at Gimont. It was late and raining hard. The prince withdrew his men to the shelter of villages in a five-mile radius and next day marshalled them for battle at first light – only to discover that the French had faded away. The divisions dispersed again, destroying as they went. Armagnac's men snapped and snarled at the English flanks and tail but nothing more. Rivers were rising and more difficult to cross; yet despite the rain there was still a shortage of water, and horses that were fobbed off with wine fell down either drunk or dead, so that the problem of transporting the booty became more acute. They captured the town of Réjaumont, luxuriated in dry lodgings after several nights spent in the open, and burned the place when they left in the morning of Friday the 27th.

There was no further opposition. The English army marched out of the county of Armagnac on Saturday 28 November. The local levies rode home with their share of the spoils. The prince was back in Bordeaux by 9 December. 'My Lord rode over the country eight whole weeks, and rested not in any place save eleven days,' Wingfield wrote. 'You may know for certain that since this war began against the French King, he never has received such loss and destruction as in this raid. For the districts and fine towns that have been laid waste in this expedition found the French King more every year, to maintain the war, than did half his realm ... Our enemies are wonderfully confounded.'

Chapter Four

✤

# The Second Chevauchée

The prince's enemies were wonderfully confounded; and wonderfully irate, too. Halting at La Réole on the march back, he allotted winter quarters to his army in fortress towns in a forty mile radius from his headquarters at Bordeaux. Salisbury was stationed at Sainte-Foy-la-Grande, on the left bank of the Dordogne below Bergerac; Warwick's men remained at La Réole, on the Garonne; most of the prince's own force were on the far bank of the Dordogne at Libourne and sharing nearby Saint-Emilion with Suffolk's troops. The prince spent ten days feasting his senior commanders, then sent them back to prepare their men for more action. The thrusts that his father had aimed at the north of France had both miscarried. Carlos of Navarre had made peace with Jean and called off Henry of Lancaster's raid in Normandy. Edward himself had sailed back from Calais to deal with the Scottish attacks in November. The French king was free to concentrate on revenging the humiliation of Languedoc. The prince must move swiftly into the second phase of his campaign – to win back the towns and fiefs around the shrunken borders of Gascony – if he was to take the best advantage of the psychological impact of that humiliation.

He advanced his personal headquarters to Libourne in the first week of January 1356, split the three battles marshalled for the *chevauchée* into smaller raiding units, and sent them fanning out to persuade the waverers and deserters to declare or renew their allegiance to his father. To the north they probed beyond the Charente, the river that marked the current limit of Gascon jurisdiction. To the north-east the Captal de Buch took the large town of Périgueux. Warwick, Chandos and others advanced up the Garonne almost as far as Agen. By early spring

King Jean had lost the allegiance of many Gascon notabilities, and the pope, asking the prince to spare Périgueux in return for a ransom, had received the same reply as had the burgesses of Carcassonne: 'that the King of England, his father, was rich ... That the Prince desired only to do that which he had set out to do, which was to punish, discipline and tame all inhabitants of the duchy of Aquitaine who had rebelled against his father.'

And not in the duchy alone. For he was about to repeat his exploit of the previous year – a great marauding raid into the territories of those who refused to submit to his father, this time not as Duke of Aquitaine but as King of France. He waited for supplies and reinforcements to be sent from England – several hundred archers, horses to carry them, bows, bowstrings and arrows for their use; salted hogs and wheat, oats and fish, so that the loyal citizens of Gascony should not complain of a shortage caused by English troops. Most of the men and material arrived by the middle of June, at which time Henry of Lancaster had landed at Saint-Vaast and was leading a lightning raid into Normandy to relieve and revictual fortresses held by the Navarrese – Carlos having once more turned against Jean.

On 25 June 1356 the prince wrote under his secret seal to the Bishop of Hereford asking him to 'command all your subjects, as well the religious as parsons, vicars and others of your jurisdiction, to go twice a week in procession, praying for us; and to pray every day for us in holy masses, by some special prayer to be appointed by you'. On 4 August, after allotting a sufficient number of men to guard the province under the command of the English Seneschal of Gascony, John de Chiverston, the prince set off from Bergerac with some 6,000 to 7,000 men, heading for the heart of France. Marching at a steady ten miles a day, deploying on either side to sear as much land as possible, up through Brantôme, Rochechouart, Châteauroux, 'they burned and destroyed all the countries they passed through; and when they entered a town that was well provisioned, they rested there some days to refresh themselves, and at their departure destroyed what remained, staving in the heads of wine casks that were full, burning wheat and oats, so that their enemies could not save anything'.

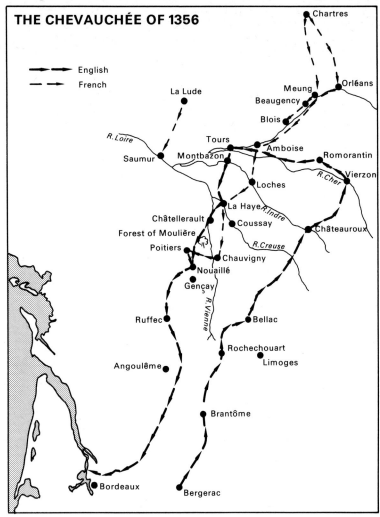

## THE CHEVAUCHÉE OF 1356

English
French

Chartres
La Lude
Meung
Beaugency
Orléans
Blois
R. Loire
Tours
Amboise
Saumur
Montbazon
Romorantin
R. Cher
Vierzon
Loches
La Haye
R. Indre
Châtellerault
Coussay
Forest of Moulière
Châteauroux
Poitiers
R. Creuse
Chauvigny
Nouaillé
Gençay
R. Vienne
Ruffec
Bellac
Rochechouart
Angoulême
Limoges
Brantôme
Bordeaux
Bergerac

Jean was determined that this raid should not be accepted as tamely as the previous year's. At Vierzon, Sir John Chandos's company met sharp resistance and prisoners were taken by each side. The prince learned that the French king was moving south with an army and had ordered additional troops to assemble at Chartres on 3 September. That same afternoon, another French detachment laid an ambush for the English vanguard. They were beaten off and took refuge in Romorantin, which lay at right angles to the route the prince had been following.

But he commanded that they should be pursued; and when they took refuge in the citadel he used all the resources of his army (which was only lightly equipped for such a task) to capture first the town, then the citadel, then the keep, with assault towers, mining and fire, 'at the which assault the Prince was personally, and by reason of his presence greatly encouraged the Englishmen'. Sieges, even if only of four or five days' duration, formed no part of a *chevauchée*. The two prisoners whom he took, Amaury Lord of Craon, King's Lieutenant in Poitou, Limousin, Saintonge and Périgord, and Jean Le Maingre called Boucicault, who later became a Marshal of France, were notable enough but not in themselves sufficient justification for the expenditure of so much effort. It seems probable that the prince decided that he had reached the farthest point of his *chevauchée* (he had covered approximately 250 miles in just under four weeks) and must return to Gascony to avoid being caught by the French king, whose army was now reported to be ten times the size of his own. But there was still a remote possibility 'of meeting with our most dear cousin the Duke of Lancaster of whom we had certain news, that he would make haste to draw towards us'. If Lancaster managed to cross the Lower Loire in time for them to form a united front they might, despite Jean's great numerical advantage, defeat him by the superior quality of their soldiers. The prince accordingly marched west along the Cher to Tours. There he raided the suburbs in the hope of tempting the garrison out to battle, while waiting three days for further news of Lancaster.

When news came, it was not of Lancaster but of Jean, who had by now crossed the Loire with his enormous army. 'So many followed him,' wrote one chronicler, 'that before he reached Orléans he had sufficient men to defeat the whole of the rest of the world.' At Orléans, Meung, Beaugency, Blois, Amboise – wherever there was a bridge – they were streaming over to the south bank of the Loire and joining the great hunting pack. Even closer at hand, units were entering Tours. Others were said to be across the Loire at Saumur, downriver. The prince had only one way to go: south. And he had to go quickly. In two days his men covered thirty miles, through Montbazon to La Haye. That night, Tuesday 13 September, Jean was a bare twenty miles away at Loches, having followed the Loire from Blois to Amboise and then turned south across the Cher and the Indre in the hope of intercepting his prey.

The prince, who had evidently intended marching along the valley of the Creuse and then probably across to the Vienne, avoiding the great French-held citadels of Poitiers and Angoulême, swung sharply back on to his original course, the modern N.10. He must have received news that Jean was approaching from the direction of Loches. He marched swiftly to Châtellerault, covering the fifteen miles in one day. There are very few clues in contemporary records to explain the moves of the two commanders, and one of the most puzzling questions of this campaign is why the prince, who up to this point seems to have been determinedly doing his utmost to elude Jean, now halted for more than two days at Châtellerault. It is just possible that he was still hoping that Lancaster might join him. It is more likely that, knowing Jean to be so close on his heels and having no opportunity of outpacing him without sacrificing his slow-moving train of booty, he decided to turn and fight it out. For this he needed to re-marshal his forces, bringing his baggage forward so that it was protected when he faced about. He needed a field suitable for battle, which he could find on the plateau north-east of Châtellerault but not in the narrow valley of the Creuse. He had reached Châtellerault in the evening of Wednesday 14 September. During Thursday he had time to array his men and to put his transport in the shelter of the town. On Friday he would expect the battle to take place.

But on Friday there was silence: no sign of Jean's vanguard advancing down the road from La Haye. It was doubtless from scouts he had sent eastward towards Coussay and La Roche-Posay that the prince belatedly learned that the French army was flooding south, on a route parallel to his own, most of it already past him. That morning, in fact, Jean was leaving Chauvigny, a good fifteen miles to the south-east. He rode west towards Poitiers, fearing that he might not be in time to intercept the prince as he came down from Châtellerault.

The prince was suddenly confronted with a hitherto unconsidered threat: that Jean's objective might not be to force a battle but to march his many thousands of men into Aquitaine in a *chevauchée* that would repay the English and Gascons in kind. The prince ordered his transport, which now blocked the

102

approaches to the bridge across the Vienne, to begin moving to the far bank immediately. By Saturday morning they were clear. He led his men-at-arms out on the Poitiers road but soon swung half-left along the fringe of the great forest of Moulière. At that moment the King of France was entering Poitiers, with his army strung out behind him along the road from Chauvigny. The end of the strange game of blind man's buff came during Saturday 18 September, when the prince's vanguard crossing the Chauvigny–Poitiers road (N.151) in a southerly direction came upon groups of the French king's rearguard riding along it to the west. Some of the Frenchmen were captured, some were killed; the remainder escaped down the road to Poitiers.

At last each commander knew where the other was. Jean turned his army round in Poitiers and massed it along the road that ran south-east to Bellac and Limoges (N.147). The prince halted his men at Sauvigny in the angle between this road and the one to Chauvigny, to regroup. He sent out strong scouting units under Bartholomew de Burghersh, the Captal de Buch and others who 'saw all the great battle of the King's; they saw all the fields covered with men of arms'. When they 'returned again to the Prince ... and said how the French host was a great number of people, "Well," said the Prince, "In the name of God let us now study how we shall fight with them to our advantage."'

Whether he decided to continue his retreat or to block the French advance, his first concern was to ensure that Jean did not cut him off from the Bordeaux road. Therefore, during Saturday evening and very early Sunday morning, he pushed his troops over the Limoges road to an open plateau just north of the village and Benedictine abbey of Nouaillé. His vanguard was commanded by the Earls of Warwick and Oxford; his rearguard by Salisbury and Suffolk. He was now a few miles southeast of the major part of the French army. To the west of Nouaillé, beyond the thickly clustered trees and the valley of the small river Miosson, a track (the modern D.142) led up through the woods to the road from Poitiers to Gençay (N.741) and from there to Ruffec on the main road to Bordeaux. He established his front along a hedge that faced north-west. He protected his right flank with a line of carts linking the hedge to the wood stretching down from the cultivated plateau to the village of Nouaillé. On his left was a gully sloping towards the Miosson, which it met opposite the hamlet of Pezay. Between Pezay and the Villeneuve bend upstream, the Miosson formed a sizeable peninsula with Boutet Wood at its southern end and a field called the Champ d'Alexandre, or Alexander's Holding, above it. From the Villeneuve marshes a lesser gully ran up to the English position. The prince ranged his archers along the hedge, supported by the men-at-arms. He was out-numbered by two or three to one – perhaps more: '1,900 men-at-arms and archers' against '7,000 men-at-arms and other much people in a huge passing number', according to one English chronicler; '3,000 men-at-arms, 2,000 archers and 1,000 "servaunts"' against '8,000 men-at-arms and 3,000 foot', according to Bartholomew de Burghersh on the English side, while the French observer, Eustace de Ribemont, estimated the prince's strength at '2,000 men-at-arms, 4,000 archers, and 1,500 others'. He had faced similar odds at Crécy ten years before; but this time the enemy was in full array before him, ready to attack, not advancing in disorder, group by group.

King Jean on this Sunday morning, 18 September 1356, heard mass in his great tent and received communion with his four sons, the nineteen-year-old dauphin, Charles Duke of Nor-mandy, the seventeen-year-old Louis Count of Anjou, the six-teen-year-old Jean Count of Poitiers and the fourteen-year-old Prince Philippe. Afterwards he held council with his nobles. 'Then finally it was ordained that all manner of men should draw into the field, and every lord to display his banner and to set forth in the name of God and Saint-Denis: then trumpets blew up through the host and every man mounted on horseback and went into the field, where they saw the King's banner wave with the wind. There might a been seen great nobles of fair harness and rich armoury of banners and pennons: for there was all the flower of France.' While this great army was being marshalled – one battle under the dauphin, one under the king's brother the Duke of Orléans, and the third and largest under Jean himself – the king sent a reconnaissance party under Eustace de Ribemont (the knight whom Edward III had rewarded with a chaplet of pearls for his courage in the Calais ambush) to 'ride on before to see the dealing of the Englishmen and advise well what number they be and by what means we may fight them, other afoot or a-horseback'.

Ribemont returned with the news that the Englishmen were few: 'Howbeit they be in a strong place, and as far as we can imagine they are in one battle.' Because of the obstacles of hedge and vines and archers, Ribemont recommended, 'Let us all be afoot, except three hundred men of arms, well horsed, of the best in your host and most hardiest, to the intent they somewhat break and open the archers, and then your battles to follow on quickly afoot and so to fight with their men of arms hand to hand.' After the stunning Crécy defeat, French military thinking had adopted the theory that – grievous though it was to their concept of chivalry – the time had now come when in any major pitched battle the man-at-arms was more effective on foot than on his horse. Since no such great battle had been fought since Crécy, there had been no opportunity for them to test this theory and learn that what was true in defence might be false in attack, and that the archers whom they continued to despise were an essential factor in each. So, 'when the French King's battles were ordered and every lord under his banner among their own men, then it was commanded that every man should cut their spears to a five foot long and every man put off their spurs'.

At this moment, when Jean was about to give the order to advance, a group of clerics came galloping from Poitiers. Their leader, Cardinal Elie Talleyrand de Périgord, begged 'that I may ride to the Prince and shew him what danger ye have him in', and thus persuade him to surrender. His request was granted. It was less than a week since they had last met, at Montbazon, where the prince had refused the cardinal's offer to arrange a truce. Now circumstances were greatly altered. The prince replied that if the terms were honourable he would gladly agree. The cardinal rode back through the vineyard to Jean, whom he asked, 'to forbear for this day until tomorrow the sun rising'. Jean, despite protests from several of his magnates who wanted to get on with the battle, agreed to the cardinal's request and set up 'a pavilion of red silk, fresh and rich' for the conference. The negotiations continued throughout the day, but there was never much hope of agreement. For the prince the truce was an invaluable breathing space, a rest

105

period for his troops after a long march with pinched stomachs. But they did not spend the day in idleness: while some took advantage of the armistice to ride along the French lines, others were digging ditches and strengthening the hedges and barricades.

There was no concealing the daunting odds they had to face. Before they settled to an uneasy rest that night, the prince addressed the archers on whose skill and fortitude so much would depend. 'Your manhood hath been always known to me, in great dangers, which showeth that you are not degenerate from true sons of Englishmen, but be descended from the blood of them ... unto whom no labour was painful, no place invincible, no ground unpassable, no hill (were it never so high) inaccessible, no tower unscaleable, no army impenetrable, no armoured soldier or whole hosts of men was formidable ... Wherefore follow your ancients and wholly be intentive to follow the commandment of your captains, as well in mind as in body, that, if victory come with life, we may still continue in firm friendship together ... But if envious Fortune (which God forbid) should let us at this present, to runne the race of all flesh, and that we end both life and labour together, be you sure that your names shall not want eternal fame and heavenly joy, and we also, with these gentlemen our companions, will drink of the same cup that you shall do.' A little later still he gave orders for Warwick to escort the baggage trucks across the Miosson. If there seemed any chance of slipping away at first light next morning he was to take them on the track through the woods to the escape road to Gençay.

The sun rose on Monday 19 September somewhere between half past five and six. Scouts from both sides were pushing forward, clashing, contending for hillocks and crests from which to observe the other's position. Warwick's men, shepherding the carts away southward, were spotted by a French patrol who galloped back and 'cried in loud voices to the King that the English were fleeing and that they would soon lose them'. With the typical indiscipline that lay at the root of so many French failures, Jean's two marshals, Arnoul d'Audrehem and Jean de

*Opposite*
Thomas
Beauchamp, 1st
Earl of Warwick.

107

Detachments of Warwick's vanguard escort the English wagons beside and through Nouaillé Wood and over the bridge at Nouaillé and the Gué de l'Orme, making for the escape road D.142. Salisbury is deployed along the hedge with the Prince of Wales in reserve. Salisbury is charged by the French cavalry under Audrehem and Clermont; the dauphin's division has dismounted to make the second wave.

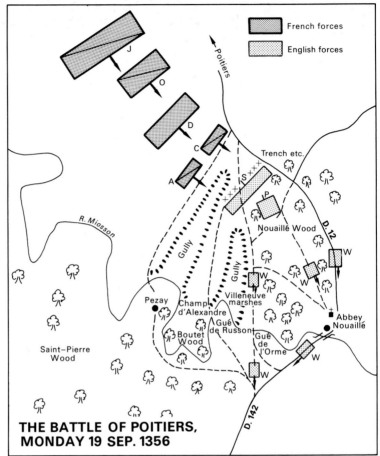

French forces

English forces

**THE BATTLE OF POITIERS,
MONDAY 19 SEP. 1356**

Clermont, now began to quarrel among themselves. Audrehem chided Clermont for being slow. Clermont, suspecting a slight upon his honour, retorted that he would so out-distance him in the attack that Audrehem would not '"come far enough forward for the point of your lance to reach my horse's rump". Thus consumed with rage they set out towards the English. Then began the uproar, the cries and clamour raised, and the armies began to draw near.'

The prince at once sent word for Warwick to return and again addressed his men: 'Now, sirs, though we be but a small company as in regard to the puissance of our enemies, let us not be abashed therefor; for victory lieth not in the multitude of people, but whereas God will send it. If it fortune that the day be ours, we shall be the most honoured people of all the world; and if we die in our right quarrel, I have the King my father and brethren, and also ye have good friends and kinsmen; these shall revenge us. Therefore, sirs, for God's sake I require you to do your devoirs this day; for if God be pleased and Saint George, this day ye shall see me a good knight.'

There was no time for more talk. The heavy cavalry of the two French marshals was thundering down on the hedge lined with Salisbury's men. The English archers began to shoot 'and did slay and hurt horses and knights, so that the horses when they felt the sharp arrows they would in no wise go forward, but drew back and flang and took on so fiercely that many of them fell on their masters, so that for press they could not rise again'.

The mounted attack collapsed. Clermont was killed; so was the Duke of Athènes, who had succeeded Bourbon as Constable of France; Audrehem was wounded and taken prisoner. With nobody of sufficient authority to rally them, the remaining horsemen fell back on the dauphin's division which was advancing on foot. Despite the resulting confusion and demoralization, the French continued their advance to the sound of 'trumpets, tabors, horns and clarions, ... banners and pennons unfurled to the wind, bright shining in gold and azure, purple, gules and ermine'. Because of the slope of the ground and the intensity of the opposition from the English archers, who 'shot swiftly, thicker than the rain falls', the French attackers bunched towards their right, thus threatening to outflank the English position on the left, where the hedge ended at the shallow gully.

Warwick, meanwhile, trying to comply with the prince's order to return from the south side of the Miosson, found the bridge and the ford below the village blocked by the baggage wagons. He was forced to cross at the Gué de Russon, on the farther side of the Villeneuve bend. Thus by good fortune he brought his men up directly to the top of the depression where the dauphin's right was about to turn Salisbury's left. Warwick's archers, extending across the depression, where the ground was too marshy for the French men-at-arms to penetrate, caught the advancing Frenchmen in the flank while his heavily armoured men attacked them from the front, 'plying

The dauphin attacks. The prince sends reinforcements to Salisbury. Warwick returns across the Gué de Russon. Orléans's men dismount ready for the third attack and, with Jean's mounted division, continue the movement southward which will outflank the English and cut their escape route.

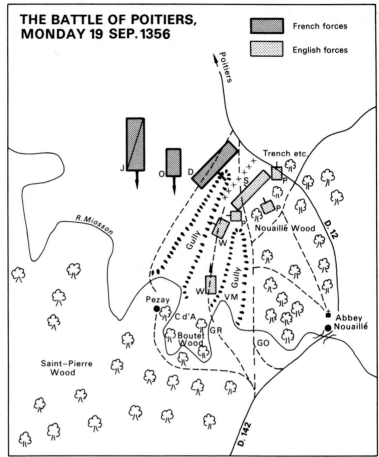

THE BATTLE OF POITIERS, MONDAY 19 SEP. 1356

French forces

English forces

the trade of arms so very chivalrously that it was truly a great marvel to behold'. The dauphin's men pressed forward, but the English line held. After a long and very bloody struggle the French began to fall back. And then, amazingly, the whole of the second French 'battle' under the king's brother, the Duke of Orléans, was seen to be mounted and moving away from the battlefield.

The reason for this mass desertion has never been discovered. Their morale must have suffered from first seeing the great cavalry charge founder on the English defences, with the death of the Constable of France and one marshal and the capture of the other, and then the failure of the dauphin's attack on

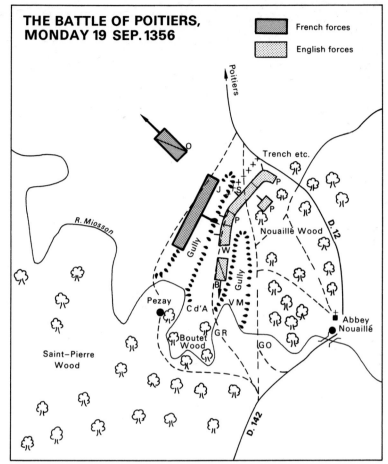

**THE BATTLE OF POITIERS,
MONDAY 19 SEP. 1356**

French forces

English forces

Poitiers

Trench etc.

R. Miosson

Nouaillé Wood

D.12

Gully

W

Gully

B

Pezay

C d'A

V M

Abbey
Nouaillé

Boutet
Wood

G R

G O

Saint–Pierre
Wood

D. 142

After the collapse
of the dauphin's
attack, Orléans's
men lose heart,
mount and ride
off the field.
Jean's division,
outnumbering
the whole
English army,
dismounts and
moves in to
attack. The
prince sends the
Capital de Buch
across the river
and into the
woods.

foot, the tactic that they had been told was the key to breaking
the English invincibility. And their spirits would not have been
raised by the news that the royal princes were being sent back to
Poitiers under a heavy guard. For King Jean, having had the
doubtful wisdom to bring his young sons to the battle, now had
the idiocy to send them openly home again – or at least to a
place of safety where too many of his supporters were already
wishing themselves to be. It was not the sort of gesture to encourage his subjects, always over-ready to dash to the field of
glory on being called heroes and away from it on suspicion that
they were dupes.

But the battle was far from over yet. During the lull, 'our

111

men carried those which were wounded to their camp and laid them under bushes and hedges out of the way; others, having spent their weapons, took the spears and swords from them whom they had overcome; and the archers, lacking arrows, made haste to draw them from poor wretches that were but half dead; there was not one of them all but either he was wounded or quite wearied with great labour.' The prince had given orders that no man should advance beyond the banner of his leader – a usual precaution for preserving the line by preventing men from running off in search of captives and ransoms. The sight of the disappearing second French division, however, was too much for the discipline of some of his men. While they scoured the plateau for French fugitives, the great host of the King of France began its advance. Because of the marshals' impetuous charge and the defection of Orléans's men, this last 'battle' had still a long distance to come. But as it approached its numbers could be seen – greater than the total English strength when the battle began and all fresh men. Beside the king rode Geoffroi de Charney, whom the prince and his father had fooled at Calais. This time he carried the *oriflamme*, the long orange pennon which proclaimed that France was in peril, the king was in command, and no prisoners would be taken.

It was a dazzling sight. Instead of following directly along the axis of the previous attacks, Jean inclined his men slightly to the south, so that, while engaging the English for the full extent of their front, he was able to use his superior numbers to advance towards the Champ d'Alexandre and thus overlap Warwick's position at the upper end of the depression leading down to the Villeneuve marsh. He was also threatening to throw his right flank across the Miosson at the Gué de Russon at the western end of the marsh, and so cut the escape road to Gençay along which the baggage carts had retreated. 'When the Prince saw him come he was somewhat amazed.' One of those nearest to him was so shocked that he blurted out: 'Alas, we poor wretches are overcome!' The prince rounded on him, shouting, 'Thou liest, thou dastardly fellow, for thou canst not say that we can be overcome as long as I live!' Yet the possibility grew stronger every minute as the French king advanced.

'They sounded their trumpets, one giving answer to another. They made such a noise that the walls of Poitiers resounded

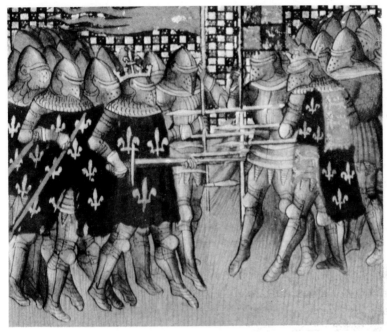

A medieval artist's impression of Poitiers: the Prince, on the right with his standard bearer, William Shank, faces King Jean and Geoffroi de Charney carrying the Oriflamme.

with the echo thereof like a wood, in such sort that a man would have thought that the hills had bellowed out to the valleys, and that the clouds had given forth a most terrible thunder ..., whilst the air shone on the bright armour and spears dashing against shining harness.

'Then came on the cruel company of crossbowmen, making a darkness in the skies with the multitude of quarrels which they shot.' Outnumbered, short of arrows, desperately tired, the English survivors closed ranks and shouted 'Guienne! St George!' in reply to the oncomers' 'Montjoie! Saint-Denis!' The prince conferred briefly with the Captal de Buch, whose troops were brigaded under Warwick in the vanguard, then sent him galloping down the hill at the head of a mixed group of mounted archers and men-at-arms. They crossed the stream and disappeared into the woods.

King Jean 'entered the battle and attacked the enemy boldly and bravely ... Now the struggle waxed sore, for the French King came up, bringing so great a power that it was a marvel to behold. When the Prince saw him, he looked up to Heaven,

113

The Captal de Buch appears at Jean's flank and rear. The prince orders his men to mount and charge.

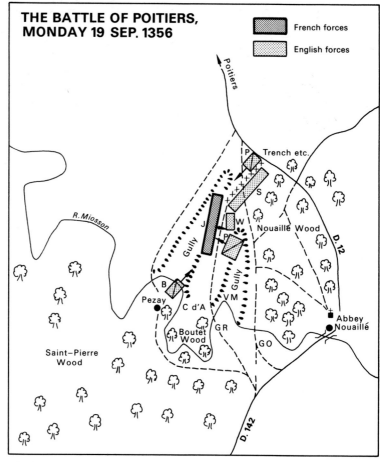

**THE BATTLE OF POITIERS, MONDAY 19 SEP. 1356**

French forces

English forces

cried mercy of Jesus Christ, and spake thus: "Mighty Father, as I believe that Thou art King above all Kings and didst endure death on the cross for us all, to redeem us out of hell, Father, who art true God, true man, be pleased by Thy most holy name, to guard me and my people from evil, even as Thou knowest, true God of Heaven, that I have good right."'

The prayer, later recorded in a rhymed Anglo-Norman biography of the prince by the herald of Sir John Chandos (who did not leave the prince's side throughout the battle), is probably something more than the usual pious interpolation in a courtly poem. The prince was a sincerely religious young man. He was also clear-sighted and bold. He was the product of a

generation of soldiers that had proved the invincibility of a com-
pact body of dismounted archers and men-at-arms against
attackers vastly superior in numbers, yet he had the independence of mind to perceive that at this stage of the long day's
battle he was no longer dealing with the Crécy equation. That
had applied to the first phase, when his archers brought down
the enemy's horses and his men-at-arms dealt with their riders.
In the second phase, with the moral advantage of a first victory
and comparative freshness, his men had just been able to swing
the scales in their favour. But now, short of arrows and physic-
ally tiring, they were at the mercy of numbers. He saw that
there was only one hope of salvation – to discard the new successful theory of defence and return to the old discredited form
of attack; to throw at King Jean's marching men the once irre-
sistible weight of armoured man on barded horse.

He had already committed himself. Staring beyond the
horde of advancing Frenchmen he saw at the back of them a
glint of steel; then a body of horsemen emerging from the west
side of Boutet Wood. At their head fluttered the red and white
banner of St George. They were the Captal de Buch's regiment
that he had sent to take the enemy in the flank and rear.

He shouted for his men-at-arms to mount. 'Let us go forth!
Ye shall not see me this day return back!' Then, to his standard-
bearer, William Shank: 'Advance, Banner, in the name of God
and of St George!' They swept round the line of archers and
spearmen and thundered into the enemy ranks. The Captal's
men charged from the rear with shouts of '"Guienne! St
George!", beating down and killing without pity; and the
archers also ... shot so thick, wounding the backs and sides of
the Frenchmen in such sort that the form of the battle was quite
spoilt, neither could they put themselves in form and array any
more.'

'There was a mighty great battle; there could you see many
a dead man ... King Jean with his own hands did that day
marvels in arms: he had an axe in his hands wherewith he
defended himself and fought in the breaking of the press.' He
was supported by the fourteen-year-old Prince Philippe, the
only one of his sons to disobey his order to quit the battlefield.
As his troops, demoralized by the attack from the rear, made
off in increasing numbers, a throng of Englishmen and Gascons,

115

eager to gain what was literally a king's ransom, gathered round the spot where his standard flew. Geoffroi de Charney was cut down at his side, 'and such as knew him cried, "Sir, yield you, or else ye are but dead."' It was unlikely that anybody would be foolish enough to kill so golden a goose, but he seemed in danger of being pulled to pieces by his would-be captors. He was saved from this by a Flemish knight in the English service – Denis de Morbeck – who 'stept forth into the press, and by strength of his body and arms came to the French King and said in good French, "Sir, yield you."' It was customary to give one's captor a piece of equipment as token of surrender. The king, having assured himself that Morbeck was of sufficiently high birth, handed him his right gauntlet (a particularly binding form of submission, because the two men could then exchange bare handclasps).

'The Prince of Wales,' said Froissart, 'who was courageous and cruel as a lion, took that day great pleasure to fight and to chase his enemies.' So also did his soldiers, released at last from the tension and pain of holding their ranks in the face of attack after attack. 'The chase endured to the gates of Poitiers;

116

'This book was taken from the King of France at Poitiers and the good Earl of Salisbury, William Montagu, bought it for 100 marks and gave it to his companion Elizabeth the good Countess.' An inscription in Jean II's illuminated Bible, now in the British Museum. After the annulment of his union with Joan of Kent, Montagu married Elizabeth Mohun.

there were many slain and beaten down, horse and man, for they of Poitiers closed their gates and would suffer none to enter; wherefore in the street before this gate was horrible murder, men hurt and beaten down. The Frenchmen yielded themselves as far off as they might know an Englishman; there were divers English archers that had four, five or six prisoners.'

Towards evening of that bloody Monday, 'the Prince did off his bassinet, and the knight for his body and they of his chamber were ready about him, and a red pavilion pight up, and then drink was brought forth to the Prince and for such lords as were about him, the which still increased as they came from the chase'. He had his banner set in the top of a tree as a rallying point and the recall sounded with trumpets and clarions. The field was strewn with the enemy dead – more than a score of dukes and counts and a hundred times as many men-at-arms. But there was one supremely important absentee from the roll-call of dead and captured: the vanquished King of France. The Prince ordered Warwick and Sir Reginald Cobham to seek news of what had become of him.

'These two lords took their horses ... and rode up a little hill to look about them. Then they perceived a flock of men of arms ...: there was the French King afoot in great peril, for Englishmen and Gascons were his masters; they had taken him from Sir Denis Morbeke perforce, and such as were most of force said; "I have taken him"; "Nay," quoth another, "I have taken him": so they strave which should have him. Then the French King, to eschew that peril, said: "Sirs, strive not: lead me courteously and my son, to my cousin the Prince, and strive not for my taking, for I am so great a lord to make you all rich."'

The promise pacified them for the moment, but then greed reasserted itself, and no doubt the conviction that possession is nine points of the law, for 'ever as they went they made riot and brawled for the taking of the King'. Warwick and Cobham, having galloped to the rescue of the badly mauled captive, were told that 'There be more than ten knights and squires that challenge the taking of him and his son'. They ordered the disputants 'to draw aback and ..., on pain of their heads, to make no more noise nor to approach the King no nearer, without they were commanded. Then ... they alighted and did their reverence to the King and so brought him and his son in peace and rest to the Prince of Wales.'

The prince entertained him to dinner. 'And always the Prince served before the King as humbly as he could, and would not sit at the King's board for any desire that the King could make, but he said he was not sufficient to sit at the table with so great a prince as the King was.' Seeing that Jean was downcast, he begged him: 'Sir, for God's sake make none evil nor heavy cheer, though God this day did not consent to follow your will. ... Methink ye ought to rejoice, though the journey be not as ye would have had it, for this day ye have won the high renown of prowess and have passed this day in valiantness all other of your party. Sir, I say not this to mock you, for all that be on our party that saw every man's deeds, are plainly accorded by true sentence to give you the prize and chaplet.'

Chapter Five

# 𝕿𝖍𝖊 𝕽𝖔𝖆𝖉 𝖙𝖔 𝕭𝖗𝖊́𝖙𝖎𝖌𝖓𝖞

It was a shattering victory. Had he chosen, the prince could perhaps have ridden to – and through – the gates of Paris; certainly
he could have laid waste a great deal more French territory.
But he and his men had gained much extra booty, and one
trophy above all that he must not let slip from his grasp – the
King of France. He therefore commanded that the retreat to
Bordeaux should continue. 'They rode but small journeys ...
and lodged over betimes; and rode close together in good
array, saving the Marshals' battles, who rode ever before with
five hundred men of arms to open the passages as the Prince
should pass; but they found no encounters, for all the country
was so frayed that every man drew to the fortresses.' They were
in Bordeaux by the first days of October, the French king sharing the prince's lodgings in the archbishop's palace beside the
cathedral, the English and Gascon troops celebrating 'in great
mirth and revel' so that, since Bordeaux was well equipped with
entertainment for jubilant fat-pursed soldiers, they had very
shortly 'spent foolishly the gold and silver they had won'.

In England 'great solemnities were made in all churches and
great fires and wakes' when King Edward announced the news
on 10 October, having probably first received it from a groom
of the prince's chamber, Geoffrey Hamelyn, who brought with
him the French king's tunic and bassinet as proof. On the 20th
the prince sent his chamberlain, Sir Nigel Loring, and another
member of his staff, Sir Roger Cotesford, to the king, the Bishop
of Worcester, and the mayor and aldermen of the City of London, with letters describing the campaign. In return he received
more wheat and oats for his men and horses, and more money,
arrows and bows. He could not yet go back to England, for

there was much administrative work to keep him occupied. He opened discussions for a truce with France. He negotiated the purchase, either on his own account or his father's, of most of the prisoners for whom the highest ransoms would be demanded. He acquired a lioness.

When the prince and King Jean signed a two year truce at Bordeaux on 23 March 1357, a great many soldiers – in Normandy and Brittany as well as in Gascony – found themselves steeped in the habits of war, accustomed to the rich rewards it could bring them, but with nobody to offer employment. They formed themselves into marauding bands known as Free Companies which for many years terrorized much of France by pillage and extortion. Soon the French chroniclers were bewailing: 'See how many towns of the kingdom are burned, how many old people butchered, young people dead by the sword, children strangled, pregnant women cleft in twain; see how many noble and distinguished virgins have served as playthings for the passions of these ferocious beasts; see how many priests and clerics of divers orders have been taken prisoner or massacred, how many churches pillaged, how many monasteries destroyed! See where horses have been stabled before the altar of the Lord, consecrated virgins defiled, holy relics cast to the winds! Even the holy sacrament has not been respected by sacrilegious hands ... France has become an object of scorn for Jews and Pagans.'

On Tuesday 11 April 1357 the prince set sail for England, with the French king and the more important French prisoners. They landed at Plymouth at the beginning of May and entered London on the 24th – the delay having given the Londoners time to decorate the streets and prepare a welcome that would dazzle the French king and honour the prince. Escorted by the mayor and aldermen, the prince brought his prisoner over London Bridge to St Paul's and out along the Strand to be received by Edward at Westminster. The houses were decked with tapestries and armorial designs, the streets were crammed with 'a great press and multitude of people, to behold and see that wonder and that royal sight'. The spectators, warmed with free wine, roared their delight at the prince's triumph and at his display of chivalrous modesty – he had mounted Jean on 'a white courser, well apparelled' while contenting himself with

Aftermath of a hunt – a man prepares to break up a stag, from a contemporary manuscript.

'a little black hobby'. Later Jean returned to the Duke of Lancaster's vast mansion, the Palace of Savoy, where he was to spend the first years of his captivity.

The prince celebrated his successful campaign with his customary lavishness: gifts of land, lump sums and annuities to close friends such as Chandos, Audley and Loring; innumerable presents of horses and armour to acquaintances and near strangers whom he met at tournaments; rare silks and brocades for religious institutions; gems and bejewelled gold and silver articles for his family and no doubt for the unidentified ladies who had borne him at least three sons; money for the gambling with which he whiled away the evenings or the days when bad weather prevented him from hunting or jousting. Both by upbringing and by character he believed that a great prince should be a great giver. And so did all who served him.

King Jean was moved from the Savoy to Windsor 'and went a-hunting and a-hawking thereabouts at his pleasure, and the Lord Philippe his son with him'. There, on St George's Day 1358, he watched the splendid tournament for which Edward gave safe conduct to all foreign knights who wished to compete, no matter what their nationality. With him in the royal stand were the gentle Queen Philippa and the ferocious Queen Isabella, now an ailing woman in her sixties. It was said that the queen-mother had regained some of her influence over Edward and was using it in favour of Jean. She had been given permission to move from Castle Rising to Hertford where her kinsman the French king (her grandfather, Philippe III, was Jean's great-grandfather) frequently visited her.

Her influence was perhaps perceptible in the treaty on which Edward and Jean 'embraced each other many times and

121

exchanged rings and dined together' early in May. Under its terms King Jean agreed to pay the enormous sum of 4 million French gold crowns for his ransom and to recognize Edward as the sovereign ruler of Aquitaine, Calais and the surrounding county of Guines, of Montreuil and the adjacent county of Ponthieu. Aquitaine was defined as extending to the northern boundary of Poitou, the eastern boundary of Quercy and down to the boundary of Bigorre along the Pyrenees. It was, except for the ransom, less than Edward had been granted under the 1354 treaty, which the French had refused to ratify; and it is probable that he shortly afterwards regretted his moderation. At the end of the month the great peasant rising of the Jacquerie threatened briefly to enlist the support of the rest of the French non-noble classes, though its violence frightened them away again; in August the francophile Queen Isabella died; in November the first instalment of Jean's ransom failed to arrive. With increased lawlessness in France, no counter-persuasion from his mother, and a sound legal excuse, Edward in December 1358 warned his admirals that he shortly intended to go with his army across the seas.

In January he formally restated his claim to the French throne. He gave Sir Thomas Holland, Joan of Kent's husband, the title of King's Lieutenant and Captain in Normandy, and ordered the mobilization of an army. The truce signed between Jean and the Prince of Wales at Bordeaux was due to run out at Easter – 21 April 1359. On 24 March Jean accepted a revised treaty, adding to the territory he had already conceded the county of Boulogne, and Normandy, Maine, Anjou and Touraine – the entire Angevin empire of Edward's Plantagenet ancestors. The ransom, though it remained at 4 million gold crowns, was in effect reduced, because it was now to cover not only Jean but also his son Philippe, the Counts of Eu and Tancarville, Marshal Audrehem and eleven other important persons. Jean was allowed to go into the country for the fine weather, occupying the apartments that had recently been Isabella's at Hertford. Edward sent out orders cancelling the mobilization.

On 19 May 1359 John of Gaunt, Earl of Richmond, was married at the royal palace at Reading to Blanche, the daughter of Henry Duke of Lancaster. The Mayor of London ordered jousts to be held in celebration of the wedding, and the king, who had a liking for such impersonations, 'privily with his four sons, Edward, Lionel, John and Edmund, and other 19 great lords, held the field' against all comers, as deputies for the twenty-four aldermen on whose behalf the challenges were issued.

They were shortly to be fighting in earnest. Because of Jean's peculiar position – Edward, though he was negotiating with him, refused to recognize him as King of France *de jure*, and, since he was a prisoner, he was not king *de facto* – all agreements needed to be ratified by the dauphin as regent and by the States General. The treaty signed in London on 24 March was taken to Paris by several notable prisoners who had instructions to bring it back signed before Pentecost (9 June). It proved unnecessary to wait that long. On Sunday 25 May 1359 the dauphin prevailed on the States General to reject the treaty as 'neither tolerable nor practicable'. It is not clear whether his motive was purely patriotic or tempered by his own ambition to keep his father prisoner in a foreign country while he continued to wield power as regent. But the States General enthusiastically voted contributions 'to make war on the Englishman' and Paris, for its own defence, undertook to provide one year's wages for '600 men-at-arms, 300 archers and 1,000 brigands' (a word which still denoted merely lightly armoured soldiers, usually mercenaries, but was soon, thanks to the Free Companies, to acquire its modern sinister meaning).

Edward once more ordered his admirals to seize all ships in port and conscript sailors to man them and carpenters to fit them out for war. King Waldemar of Denmark (who had claims to the English throne because of his descent from William the Conqueror) proposed invading England with 12,000 men, rescuing Jean and restoring Owen, grand-nephew of Llewelyn, the last Welsh Prince of Wales, if the dauphin would contribute 600,000 florins to the cost of the expedition. King Jean was transferred under a strong guard to Somerton Castle near Lincoln. For a gift of lands and the promise of 600,000 gold crowns over twelve years, Carlos of Navarre called off his quarrel with the dauphin and undertook to defend France against the English.

In England, the first detachments of soldiers were directed

to be at Sandwich by 4 August. The Prince of Wales moved down to nearby Northbourne Manor, having guaranteed his creditors first lien on four years' revenues from his states if he were killed in battle. The sheriffs collected stores and directed them to river towns from which they were sent in small boats to the ports to be transferred to seagoing vessels – flour, oats, salt pork, mutton, beef, cheese, dried peas and beans, bows at 16d to 18d each, arrows at about the same price for a sheaf of twenty-four (approximately 13d for the feathered shafts and 3d for the steel heads – prices varied from place to place because of the cost of carriage), bowstrings at 3s a gross. Wheelwrights and others were set to making carts to carry the stores. Because this was to be a very large expedition, the county bow-makers, fletchers and armourers could not supply all the weapons the king required; the royal arsenal at the Tower of London engaged more craftsmen to fill the gap, and ordered extra supplies of yew and ash, horse-hair and hemp, iron and charcoal, sulphur and saltpetre.

On 28 October, 'between dawn and sunrise, the King embarked in a ship called the *Philip* of Dartmouth in the port of Sandwich and, having set sail, passed thence to Calais with the Lords and other Magnates, and arrived there about the hour of vespers'. It was a dramatic arrival. The king was accompanied by Edward Prince of Wales, Lionel Earl of Ulster, John Earl of Richmond and Edmund of Langley: the martial patri-

Weapons being transported by horse and cart. The helmet carried by the second rider resembles that of the Earl of Warwick.

arch parading to war with four of his handsome, valiant sons. Obscurely, in the Earl of Ulster's retinue, went a young man of nineteen with a gift for versifying, who had been the countess's page and was looking for advancement on the fringes of the court: Geoffrey, the son of a London wine merchant named John Chaucer. On 4 November 1359 the king marched out of Calais. In his baggage train were 6,000 carts, handmills for grinding captured corn and ovens for baking the flour into bread, forges for repairing arms and armour and shoeing horses, tents and ornate pavilions for the magnates, three-man collapsible leather boats for fishing, thirty falconers with their hawks, and 120 couples of hounds and harriers so that the king might go hunting every day.

The Prince of Wales and the Duke of Lancaster commanded the second and third battles. Observers noted the discipline that the prince maintained in his order of march; permitting no stragglers, he 'rode a soft pace ready ranged in battle as though they should incontinent have fought'. The ability to keep a close but light-handed control on his disparate forces was one of his greatest qualities as a commander. As they passed out of the Calais pale and deeper into French territory the three columns moved parallel on a front some ten miles wide, burning and plundering as they went.

They found this time that they had often been forestalled. The dauphin – 'that lawyer' as John of Gaunt contemptuously called him – was determined to avoid the disasters of Crécy and Poitiers, even though this meant enduring the miseries of an unopposed *chevauchée*. He gave instructions for all those who could to take refuge in the towns and to leave nothing in the countryside that would be of value to the English. It was a systematic application of the scorched earth policy that had been pursued piecemeal during previous invasions. The great carts, each drawn by three or four horses, remained empty instead of creaking under the loads of corn and oats that Edward had counted on capturing to eke out his own supplies. Villages and farm buildings were burned as the English rode through Artois and Picardy, but there was little in the way of loot. They skirted round the cities that lay in their path – Saint-Quentin, Laon – for Edward had a set objective this time. He was making for Rheims and the cathedral where the Kings of France had traditionally been crowned since Clovis was received into Christianity there in 496, a hundred years before Augustine arrived in England.

On Wednesday 4 December 1359 Edward set up his headquarters outside Rheims in the Benedictine abbey at Saint-Basle, ten miles south of the city, with the Duke of Lancaster to the north at Brimont. The Prince of Wales's division was based at Villedomange, five miles to the south-west. The king may have expected Rheims to surrender immediately he arrived, for the archbishop, Jean de Craon, had been an outspoken opponent of the dauphin during the constitutional troubles after Poitiers and was known to have boasted of his kinship with Edward (exceedingly remote – he was descended from a daughter of John Lackland's widow). But it soon became apparent that the archbishop had changed allegiance – and that the town's defences had been greatly strengthened. For the first time since Calais, the English sealed off a town and settled down to a formal blockading siege. But it was cold; rain fell almost continually and often in torrents. At Cormicy the prince captured the castle by escalading the walls, and when the keep refused to surrender he brought up his engineers, who mined and destroyed it. Lancaster went off with some of his men to raid north-eastward towards the Ardennes. At Réthel young Geoffrey Chaucer was taken prisoner, and held in captivity until March 1360, when the king contributed £16 to his ransom.

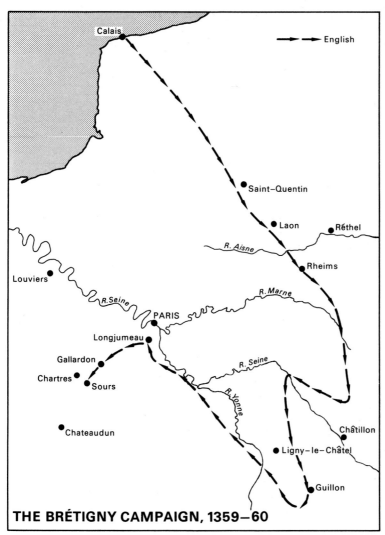

**THE BRÉTIGNY CAMPAIGN, 1359—60**

In Paris the dauphin fell ill. Temperamentally unequipped to relieve the tensions of conflict by martial exercise like Edward and the Prince of Wales, he lost his hair, his fingernails and the use of his right hand, and fretted himself into abscesses. Yet his tactics were succeeding. The English, though foraging all over the countryside around Rheims, were facing a shortage of food. Edward rightly refused to mount a direct assault on the town with its attendant heavy casualties. On 11 January

127

1360 he raised the siege and withdrew – but not in the direction of Calais. Redeploying his three columns, he rode south, across the Marne, across the Seine, ravaging the county of Champagne, untouched by previous *chevauchées* and unprepared for one now. Suddenly there was food for all, time for feasting, for hunting with the hawks and hounds they had brought from England, and for fishing from the collapsible leather boats.

The prince kept to the west of his father's route and at Ligny-le-Châtel some of his detachments were attacked by local guerrilla bands. The French regular troops were less formidable: 'Five English esquires belonging to the army of the Prince, without armour except their helmets and shields, having only one coat-of-mail, and three archers, were in a cornmill not far from Auxerre. Fifty men-at-arms came to attack them; but the five defeated the fifty, taking eleven prisoners; wherefor even the French of the other garrisons called this in mockery the exploit of fifty against five.'

'In my youth the Britons, who are called Angles or English, were reputed to be the most timid of barbarians,' wrote Petrarch, who had been on an embassy from the Viscontis to the French court, 'but now they are the most warlike of peoples. They have overthrown the ancient military glory of France by such numerous and unexpected victories that those who were not long since inferior to the miserable Scots . . . have so devastated the whole realm with fire and sword that on a recent journey I had difficulty in convincing myself that it was the same France that I used to know.' Or, as the impious were heard to say: 'The Pope is a Frenchman, but Jesus has become an Englishman.'

The young Duke of Burgundy and his council (he was thirteen and a half years old) determined that Burgundy should be spared the miseries that had been visited on the rest of France. Edward, playing upon the traditional rift between Burgundy and the French crown, had noticeably restrained his troops when they entered the duchy. They took whatever they wanted, but they did not destroy what was left. The Burgundian representatives met Edward at his headquarters at Guillon and agreed to pay him to march away – the very substantial sum of 200,000 *moutons d'or*. On 15 March 1360 he rode out of Burgundy, swinging west and then north-west. This again was territory that the English army had not so far ravaged, and at the end of the journey lay the possibility that he might tempt or shame the dauphin into coming out to fight. The weather turned 'as fair, gentle, pleasant and warm as anybody could remember it' so early in the year.

Edward jogged along the course of the Yonne, spreading out across the pasture and woodlands of the Gâtinais, possibly intending to exploit the fertile plains that lay between him and Normandy. But at some point, probably not more than a week after he left Burgundy, he received news which 'so exasperated and provoked him that he immediately turned his army towards Paris . . ., burning, slaying and devastating everywhere'. The tempo and the temper of the march changed violently. 'He commanded his host to destroy and slay with dint and strength of sword those that he had beforehand spared.' As far away as Scotland it was reported that Edward, who usually showed marked respect for religious properties, 'reduced to an endless waste even the noblest monasteries, and other stately places of sundry religious orders, as well as abbeys of nuns, after having destroyed all their substance upon earth. No one in the French Kingdom durst lift his head against him.'

The information which drove Edward into this fit of black fury was that, at the moment when he was successfully holding Burgundy to ransom, the dauphin had struck a dramatic blow against him in England. On Sunday 15 March 1360 a French fleet landed 1,200 men-at-arms and 800 crossbowmen at Winchelsea. There were provisions to cope with such an attack. All men living within seven leagues of the sea were liable for service with the coastguard, which kept watch, gave the alarm by lighting beacons, and rallied the men to assembly points to repel the invaders. But it was twenty years since French troops last set foot in England. The unpractised coastguard reacted overexcitedly. Although the French withdrew the following day, the message that reached London and the king was that they were 'riding over the country, slaying, burning, destroying and doing other mischief'.

Edward marched to within twenty miles of Paris and set his headquarters at Chanteloup, near Arpajon, on 31 March, the Tuesday before Easter, his right flank on the Seine near Corbeil and his vanguard before Longjumeau, less than thirteen miles

Knighthood
conferred on the
field of battle, by
the simple laying
on of hands and
accolade.

from the capital. From here the raiding detachments spread
west and north. 'All the people fled in terror and took shelter.'
On Easter Monday the French authorities gave instructions for
the deserted suburbs of Paris to be set on fire, so that they should
not provide cover for an English assault. The dauphin Charles
ordered his troops to remain within the city walls.

Simon de Langres, General of the Preaching Friars, who had
been attempting to arrange a truce ever since Edward began
his campaign five months before, had managed to bring representatives of the two sides together at a lazar-house outside
Longjumeau on Good Friday, 3 April 1360. The talks broke
down. Edward moved his headquarters up to Châtillon, with
the Prince of Wales's advanced parties marauding as far as
Vanves, Montrouge and Gentilly, only three and a half miles
from the dauphin's palace in the centre of the city. The English
knights hurled defiance and taunts at the Frenchmen whom

they accused of skulking like cowards behind the fortifications. There was no reply. Edward, who had failed to reduce Rheims, was certainly incapable of successfully assaulting Paris. When he exposed his vulnerable baggage columns in the inevitable confusion of withdrawal the French would be able to harass them safely and effectively.

On 10 April another truce conference was arranged, this time by the Abbot of Cluny near Montrouge. It was fruitless. Two days later, on the Sunday, Paris was awakened by a new and even more violent demonstration. 'The Prince of Wales . . ., who commanded the advance guard,' wrote Sir Thomas Gray, 'and the Duke of Lancaster with another column, marched close under the faubourgs from sunrise till midday and set them on fire.' It was not until they moved away that the defenders realized that, under cover of the demonstration, Edward had marshalled the main body of his troops and was miles along the road to Chartres. The French had been cheated of their expected opportunity to attack the English baggage train. To complete their discomfiture they now fell into a trap laid for them by the Prince of Wales as he and the Duke of Lancaster withdrew. 'Knights of the Prince's retinue, newly dubbed that day, concealed themselves among the suburbs when the said columns marched off, and remained there till some came out of the city, then spurred forth and charged them.' The Frenchmen were driven back within the walls, shocked and shaken.

The territory through which Edward led his men had been despoiled almost without respite by the Free Companies. According to Froissart his plan was to strike down to the Loire valley, follow the river west to Brittany (where he could call upon the Montfort faction for support and supplies) and rest his men there until the autumn before returning to threaten Paris. He may equally well have intended to cross the Loire and continue through Poitiers to Bordeaux. Certainly his troops must have been eager for a rest from campaigning and a chance to enjoy their spoils – meagre though they were in comparison with the Prince of Wales's great success five years before. 'On Sunday the 13th of April it became necessary to make a very long march towards Beauce by reason of want of fodder for the horses. The weather was desperately bad, with rain, hail and snow, and so cold that many weakly men perished in the field.'

The troops' morale was not improved when, on the second day's march, they were overtaken by a frightening storm at the cross-roads at Gallardon, between the forest of Rambouillet and Chartres. 'Suddenly there came a horrible tempest of thunder and lightning, and afterwards hail, and it killed men without number and more than six thousand horses.' The figure is an evident exaggeration, but it well expresses the terror of the day which the troops nicknamed Black Monday: 'such a storm and tempest that none of our nation heard nor saw never none such.'

A fortnight later, on the road to Chateaudun, Edward was overtaken by ambassadors from Paris, with further offers of peace. The dauphin, faced with a new wave of the bitter dis-content that had already found expression in the peasants' revolt of the Jacquerie and a bourgeois revolution in Paris under Etienne Marcel, could not risk laying his countrymen open to further English raids. What terms he had offered at the two previous meetings is not known, but since the Duke of Lancaster, who led the English delegation at both of them, urged the king to consider favourably this third approach, it would seem that the dauphin had made some new concessions. His latest proposals were roughly those of the agreement signed by his father in May 1358. Edward turned back and set up his headquarters at Sours. On Friday 11 May 1360 definitive talks began at Brétigny, midway between Sours and Chartres. A week later, agreement was complete.

Edward renounced his claims to the crown of France and to the former Plantagenet possessions of Anjou, Maine, Touraine and Normandy. In return he was to hold Aquitaine – Gascony, Guienne, Poitou, Saintonge, Agenais, Périgord, Limousin, Quercy, Tarbes, Bigorre, Gaure, Angoumois, Rouergue – and in the north Ponthieu, Montreuil, Calais, Guines, 'in all freedom and perpetual liberty, as sovereign lord and liege and as neighbour to the Kings and realm of France, without recognising the King or Crown of France as sovereign nor paying any homage, obedience, appeal, subjection to him, nor in any future time rendering him any service or recognition'.

King Jean's ransom was reduced to 3 million gold crowns, the first instalment of 600,000 to be paid within four months of Jean's arrival under escort at Calais, which Edward promised should not be later than three weeks after the feast of St John the Baptist (24 June). Jean would be freed as soon as the first instalment had been paid and forty of the greatest French lords (including Jean's two sons, Louis Duke of Anjou and Jean Count of Poitiers, now Duke of Berry, who would thus join his youngest, Philippe, in captivity) had surrendered as hostages, to be followed within three months by four of the richest citizens of Paris and two from each of eighteen other large towns. To ensure the continuance of peace, the two kings would renounce their present alliances – France with Scotland, England with Flanders – and do their utmost to resolve fairly the quarrel of the conflicting claimants to the duchy of Brittany, which Edward now recognized as a fief of the French crown.

Six English knights journeyed to Paris, where the dauphin was immobilized by an abscess, to witness his signature to the treaty on 10 May. The following morning they left with six French knights who were to see the Prince of Wales sign on behalf of Edward. They found him at Louviers, between Evreux and Rouen, for the bulk of the English army was now withdrawing to Calais, while the royal headquarters struck off towards Honfleur and the shortest route home. The treaty would not be finally ratified by the two kings until Jean was released at Calais. In the meantime the prince still signed as 'son of the noble king of France and of England'.

Edward and his four sons rode in triumph into Westminster in the evening of 19 May 1360. Edward ordered six weeks of feasting, which reached their climax on 14 June, when, with the Prince of Wales, he entertained King Jean to a banquet at the Tower of London, Jean having that day provisionally ratified the treaty. On the 30th the Prince of Wales escorted Jean in a leisurely progress to Dover, where they arrived on Monday 6 July. While the prince was entertaining him to dinner at the castle, a squire arrived from London bringing a goblet as a parting gift from Edward. The open-handed Jean sent Edward in return his own goblet, the famous hanap that had once belonged to Saint Louis, and rewarded the messenger with the princely sum of thirty nobles. (The gold crown, franc, florin, *livre tournois*, or *mouton d'or* – so called because it had an impression of the *Agnus Dei* on one side – all had a nominal value of

3s 4d, or £0·166666 ... in our more practical modern coinage. The noble, struck to commemorate Edward's victory at Sluys, showed him standing in a ship and was worth two crowns. The mark was worth four crowns, the pound sterling six. In 1934 Dr Coulton reckoned that medieval moneys should be multiplied by forty to give their modern equivalents. If this book passes speedily through the press the present-day multiplier may be estimated at not much more than three hundred.)

Jean sailed for Calais early in the morning of 8 July and arrived before nightfall. He had to await the collection of his ransom. Arrangements had already been made for money raised from a special tax to be sent to Saint-Omer. The pope, two years before, had instructed the French bishops to subscribe two tithes (which the dauphin, for his own dark reasons, now ordered should be only one). The burgesses and other commons of the kingdom, according to Jean de Venette, 'greatly desired the return of King Jean, so that when he came back the vicious noblemen ... might be brought to justice'. But their eagerness did not appreciably loosen their pursestrings and Jean might have had to wait a long time had he not agreed to the wedding of his youngest daughter, eleven-year-old Isabelle, to Gian Galeazzo, son of one of the Viscontis of Milan. The Viscontis paid Jean 100,000 florins when the marriage documents were signed and another 500,000 when the bride arrived at Milan on 9 October. Together they were the exact amount of the first instalment of Jean's ransom.

That same day the Prince of Wales, who had crossed to Calais in August, welcomed his father, who had come over for the final ratification of the treaty. In a fortnight of many solemnities, former enemies were reconciled, the dauphin arrived from Boulogne to dine with his father and Edward, and the Treaty of Brétigny was discussed at great length by Edward's lawyers and those brought by the dauphin. There was difficulty over a part of clause 11 and the whole of clause 12, under which the two kings renounced their claims to Aquitaine on the one hand and Normandy, Touraine, etc., on the other. The precise nature of the difficulty did not seem clear to anybody except the dauphin's lawyers. Jean himself was evidently ready to sign the treaty as it stood, in order to regain his liberty. But, since Edward had no objection (his garrisons were in control of the territories concerned), it was agreed that these two clauses should be extracted and form a new and separate treaty to be ratified when the remaining conditions of the first treaty had been complied with – the date and place for this, too, was agreed upon: the feast of St Andrew (30 November) 1361.

On Saturday 24 October 1360 the two kings took their places in tented 'oratories' erected for them in the choir of the church of Saint-Nicolas. The papal legate, the abbot of Cluny, celebrated mass. Then, while the chancellors of the two countries – William Edington, Bishop of Winchester, amd Gilles Aycelin de Montaigu, Bishop of Thérouanne – held the open gospels between them, the legate invited Edward and Jean to kneel at the altar steps and swear upon the consecrated host to observe the conditions of the treaty.

To the surprise of the onlookers, Edward turned to Jean and said: 'Good brother! Take heed that you observe loyally and well all the matters touched upon and agreed between us and you, between our councils and yours . . ., because otherwise we do not desire or intend to swear any oath; and in the event of our having so sworn, it is not and shall not be our will or intention to be bound to any thing or in any manner; and only as far as you keep and faithfully observe towards us all the things promised and agreed on your part, shall we hold and keep loyally and well what we have promised or sworn.' Nor was he satisfied with Jean's repeated assurances, but demanded a notarized copy of the proceedings after both had taken the oath. Jean's three sons, Louis, Jean and Philippe, followed him in swearing to observe the peace, as did the Prince of Wales and his two brothers. And both parties agreed that 'we shall ensure that the same oath is taken, as soon as may well be done, by the greater part of the prelates, peers, dukes, counts, barons and other nobles of our realm'.

Edward's strange outburst, and the elaborate guarantees and promises upon which he insisted, revealed a deep suspicion that the French somehow intended to cheat him. His presentiment was well founded. The architect of this deception was not present at Calais; he had returned to Boulogne – the harbinger of a new age in which intellectual cunning would triumph over physical strength, Renaissance Man confronting, or outflanking, Medieval Man. The great innovation of the 1300s – though

'A gentle knight who had but one eye, who was called Sir Thomas Holland' – portrayed here after fulfilling his vow to wear a white eye-patch until he had performed deeds of valour in France.

the century was over before men were aware of it – was the use of gunpowder in war, so that an undersized artilleryman was now to be more than a match for the strong-armed bowman or the giant in armour. Just so did the despised 'Lawyer' Charles of France, gouty, rheumatic, consumptive, painfully thin, a creature of innumerable ailments, acne, abscesses and alopecia, triumph over the Lion of England and his fierce tall sons.

For the moment the surface of the new peace was unruffled, though the portents were far from favourable. In England at this time 'men, beasts, trees and housing perished with sudden tempest and strong lightning; and the Devil appeared bodily in man's likeness to many people as they went in divers places in the country and spoke to them'. Jean left Calais and captivity for Boulogne on Sunday 25 October 1360, accompanied two or three miles by Edward and all the way by the Prince of Wales. On Monday the prince and the dauphin exchanged vows to keep the peace. On Tuesday the first instalment of Jean's ransom fell due and, despite the price he got for his daughter, he produced only 400,000 gold crowns. Edward agreed to let the remaining 200,000 stand over until the last week of December and proceeded with his side of the bargain by ordering Sir Thomas Holland, his lieutenant-general in Normandy, to begin withdrawing the English garrisons from the duchy and from Anjou and Maine. Edward and his sons sailed back to Dover on 31 October, accompanied by thirty of their highborn hostages, ten having been released on payment of the first instalment of the ransom. While the others rode on to London, the Prince of Wales remained at Canterbury for almost a week, praying before the shrine of St Thomas in the Trinity Chapel.

In the last days of the year, Sir Thomas Holland died, a founder knight of the Order of the Garter, one of the most famous chivalrous figures in Europe, and still better known as Holland than as Earl of Kent, the title he had inherited on the death of his wife's brother. The silver rampant lion on his azure banner powdered with lilies had stood in the thick of the fray against the French in Aquitaine, Flanders, Brittany and Normandy, at Crécy and at Calais. He had fought against the Spaniards in the great sea-battle off Winchelsea, against their infidel invaders, the Moors of Granada, and against the heathen Prussians in far-off Baltic lands. He left three sons and two daughters and a beautiful widow – the thirty-two-year-old Fair Maid of Kent, the former Countess of Salisbury in whose honour the king had founded the Order of the Garter.

In February 1361, the prince was present with his father and brothers at Westminster when each member of Parliament took the oath to preserve the peace with France. In April he journeyed to Leicester to place two cloths of gold on the bier of the great Duke of Lancaster who had died in a recurrence of the plague. In May he was back in London, preparing for marriage. For the Prince of Wales, on the verge of his thirty-first birthday, had at last found a bride.

# Chapter Six

# Prince of Aquitaine

The most eligible bachelor in England – and all Europe – had made a surprising choice: 'his cousin the Lady Jeanette', Countess of Kent. According to a French chronicle written during the last twenty years of the fourteenth century, after Holland's death there was such competition to marry his widow that 'many noble knights who had greatly served the King of England and the Prince his son, came to ask the Prince to speak to the Countess on their behalf'. The prince agreed to the request of one named Brocas. But when he approached his cousin she – 'who was subtle and wise' – replied that she would never marry again. As he persisted in pleading Brocas's cause, 'the Prince was greatly overcome with love for the Countess'. She began to weep. 'Then the Prince took her in his arms to comfort her, and he kissed her many times, his heart touched by her tears.' She begged him not to press her to marry Brocas. 'For I am devoted to the most valiant man on earth … and it is impossible for me to have him.' When the prince urged her to say who it was, she at last confessed, '"It is you – and for love of you no other knight shall ever be at my side." Then the Prince, greatly consumed with love, said: "I swear to God that as long as you live I shall have no other woman than you."'

This story of sudden infatuation and calculated enticement is unlikely not only because it does not chime with the character of the prince, but also because he knew Joan well, saw her often, and was even said by gossips to have already been her lover.

The quite strong breath of scandal – she was popularly believed to have been divorced by Salisbury because of misconduct with Holland, and the garter affair was taken as proof that she had been the mistress of her foster-father Edward (gossip on the Continent accused him of having originally seduced her by force) – made her an unlikely and scarcely acceptable bride for the heir apparent. The pope disapproved on the grounds of consanguinity – she was the prince's first cousin once removed and he had stood as godfather to two of her five children. The Archbishop of Canterbury, Simon Islip, warned him that because of Joan's divorce from Salisbury (who was still alive) the legitimacy of any children of her marriage to the prince might be challenged – a prediction amply fulfilled before the end of the century when the London mob screamed 'bastard!' at Richard II. There was the added oddity, for a royal marriage, that his wife was a twice married widow and divorcée and two years older than he.

There is consequently one aspect of this rather mysterious affair about which there can be no doubt at all: the prince was profoundly in love with the slim, graceful Countess of Kent. He had been under great pressures, as heir to the throne, to marry young and protect the succession by sons of his own. That he had so long withstood them, and now married the countess so soon after her widowing, suggests that he may have loved – and waited for – his dear Lady Jeanette since their childhood. 'For he could have married much higher, and there was not an Emperor, King or Prince beneath heaven, who would not have been overjoyed if the Prince of Wales had entered his family.' Jeanette was, like the prince, lavish with money – for clothes and jewels and furniture and friends. To celebrate her marriage she had made a bed of red velvet decorated with his ostrich feathers in silver, leopards' heads in gold. Where he was forceful, she was gentle and kindly, blushing repeatedly if people praised her radiant loveliness. The perils of childhood, the execution of her father for treason, had left her with a more than common fear of insecurity, yet she could summon up deep reserves of courage, as she had shown when she directed the defence of Wark Castle in her teens. But it was as a beautiful warm-hearted woman, 'que bele fu plesant et sage – lovely, pleasant and wise', as Sir John Chandos's herald described her, that most people remembered her. 'One of the loveliest women in the world,' said the French author of the *Chronicle of the Four First Valois Kings*.

Joan of Kent, depicted in a manuscript from the Abbey of St Albans of which she and the Prince were both benefactors. *Opposite* The Black Prince from the same manuscript, with Edward III directly above.

The wedding contract was signed at the archbishop's palace at Lambeth on 6 October 1361, and the regally handsome couple were married at Windsor on Sunday the 10th. That Christmas they entertained the royal family at Berkhamsted, the honeymoon home which they scarcely left from late November until the spring of 1362. But the king's sense of outrage at his son's choice of bride, and his own unusual relationship with his daughter-in-law, made it advisable to place as much distance as possible between the two households. By the summer Edward had found a solution to the problem: the prince and his beautiful but embarrassing wife were to be sent into very honourable exile. He was to return to Gascony, the scene of his greatest triumph. This time, however, his title was not that of king's lieutenant, but the far grander one of Prince of Aquitaine. Apart from the token ounce of gold which he was to pay as tribute each Easter as an acknowledgement of his father's suzerainty and right to decide the succession, the prince was to rule as a king, striking his own coinage, appointed for life.

There was no undignified haste in getting rid of the prince.

141

His letters of appointment were dated 19 July 1362 but it was almost twelve months before he arrived at Bordeaux. He remained in England to join in the lavish celebrations for his father's fiftieth birthday on 13 November 1362; he once more entertained his parents at Berkhamsted at Christmas, and did not reach his new capital until June 1363, having landed at La Rochelle and made a royal progress south. Though the Rochellois had written to the King of France 'saying how they had rather be taxed yearly to the half of their substances than to be under the hands of the Englishmen', the majority of the prince's subjects were in no mood to complain. Their former rights were re-confirmed, their ancient institutions preserved. They lost no privileges by ceasing to be governed by the King of France, and gained one new and precious advantage – security. Protected by the constable, Sir John Chandos, and now by the towering reputation of the prince himself, they had little to fear from the Free Companies which were still marauding almost unopposed across the border in France. As for the nobility and martial gentry, there was this advantage in siding with the English: that plunder could be taken from the French. In fighting for the French it was only Gascony, not England, that could be looted.

They were flattered to have so famous a man among them and delighted with the way he accepted their homage. 'The Earls, Viscounts, Barons and Knights of Gascony were received right joyously, and the Prince acquitted himself so nobly among them that every man was well content.' It is a recurring comment: 'The Prince lovingly received them, as he could right well do ... There was no Prince in his time could show more honour than he.' He had the dignified, warm friendliness of a man of proven courage and undisputed rank. And there was his renowned princely largesse in the bestowal of money and other gifts. As for the entertainment his subjects received at the court of Aquitaine: 'the state of the Prince and the Princess was so great that in all Christendom was none like.' At these great feasts of mutton and veal and venison, goose and rabbit, sucking pig, lampreys, peacocks and oysters (and cats and dogs, blackbirds and hedgehogs, though not perhaps on the most formal occasions), the enormous *Salles* or Halls of tapestry were brought out: richly embroidered lengths of cloth that covered

142

all the walls of the banqueting chamber, eight pieces for the sides, an especially ornate 'dosser' to hang behind the prince and two 'bankers' for the benches at the high table. They were of many colours and designs, but his favourites were black with silver ostrich plumes and the edging of swans with women's heads which decorated nearly all.

It was at this period that he incorporated in his seal the ostrich feathers that became the badge of successive Princes of Wales (though his spelling of the German motto 'I serve' was *ich dene*, not the modern *ich dien*). There is no evidence that this was ever the badge of the blind King of Bohemia from whom legend says that the Prince captured it at Crécy. Neither is there any historical support for the sixteenth-century story that he wore black armour at Crécy. He gave pieces of black armour to his friends, he chose a sable field to display the silver plumes on his banner, the costliest tapestries of his palaces were predominantly black. He liked the colour and made much use of it – and that is at the moment the most probable explanation of why he was called (though never in his lifetime, as far as is known) the Black Prince.

He immediately issued new coins with his own name on them – assurances of a stable monetary policy and good trade. There were already signs that it had been high time for him to take up his post. In July 1361, King Jean had presided at a trial by battle between two knights named Foulque d'Archiac and Maingot Maubert. The contest took place at the Market of Meaux, a fortified field in a loop of the Marne above Paris, on so torrid a day that Foulque, who fell off his horse and continued to fight on foot, was often compelled to sit down on a bench at the end of the lists to recover his strength. Maingot, who remained mounted and should have scored an easy victory, lost the contest by collapsing over the pommel of his saddle, dead of heat-stroke. The details, unusual though they were, were of less interest than the fact that both the knights were Gascons. Edward promptly lodged a vigorous protest against Jean's presumption of jurisdiction over subjects of Aquitaine: a flagrant breach of the Treaty of Brétigny. Jean replied that he had exercised no judicial functions – that there were precedents for knights choosing as their referee in trial by battle a person of accepted authority not necessarily the superior to

Edward III invests
his eldest son with
the Principality of
Aquitaine.

whom they would appeal for judgement on a point of law. Even
if that were true, it was a stupidly tactless action in the circumstances, and one that Edward reasonably suspected to be the
thin end of an oath-breaking wedge.

The suspicion hardened when Jean defaulted on the instalment of his ransom for 1361 (he was committed to six annual
payments of 400,000 crowns to complete the total of 3 million).
He prevailed on the pope to send the Abbot of Cluny, now a
cardinal, to England to propose a reduction, but Edward, in-

Edward of
Woodstock's Privy
Seal as Prince of
Aquitaine: one of
the earliest
examples of his use
of the ostrich
feathers.

creasingly distrustful of French cardinals, French popes and
French kings, flatly refused – and rightly declined to release any
of the hostages he had brought back from Calais. In the autumn
of 1362 Jean went to Avignon for personal discussions with the
pope. By the time he arrived, Innocent VI had died and had
been succeeded by another Frenchman, Guillaume de Gri-
moard, as Urban V, who refused to lend Jean money for the
payment of his ransom and suggested instead that he should
lead a crusade which Urban offered to finance. For this the

pope would hire the Free Companies and thus rid Europe of the pest of roving mercenaries while forwarding his Christian vocation of slaughtering infidels. The proposal had attractions for Jean. If he went on a crusade his debts would be suspended and his affairs taken under the protective wing of Holy Mother Church.

Jean returned to Paris in May 1363 having accepted the post of captain-general of the crusade, which was to leave on the first day of March 1365. About the same time, the four royal hostages – his sons Anjou and Berry, his brother Philippe of Orléans, and his cousin Louis of Bourbon – arrived at Calais as the result of a bargain they had struck with Edward. Despite the arrears of payment of Jean's ransom it was agreed that the four hostages should be given restricted release in return for 200,000 crowns and the confirmation of Edward's rights over some townships. While they waited in Calais for the money to be collected they were allowed to make visits outside the English pale for periods of not more than four days.

This was the situation when the Prince of Wales, having received oaths of fealty from his Gascon lords at Bordeaux, progressed to his palace at Poitiers to keep an eye on those parts of the principality that had most recently been French. Here he learned that the king's elder son, Louis Duke of Anjou, having been given permission to go on pilgrimage to Notre-Dame-de-Boulogne, had there met his wife Marie de Châtillon, gone with her to Guise, and refused to return to Calais. To the prince this news came as a great shock. He was aware of the untrustworthiness of the French, but his strict code of honour made it almost impossible for him to believe that a knight –

and a king's son – could break such a solemn oath as Anjou had
taken: that if he or his companions did not return, 'we desire
that we shall be held and reputed as forsworn and guilty of
false faith in all places and before all lords and persons'.

In an uneasy peace 1363 drifted icily into 1364. It was the
coldest winter in living memory, and one of the longest. The
Seine was frozen over from Christmas to February, the Rhine
from January to March; carts were driven across the Rhône
and the Meuse; on the Mediterranean coast the Bassin de Thau
became a thick sheet of ice. A horse plodded up to an inn at
Carcassonne with its rider frozen dead in the saddle; fortresses
were suddenly stripped of half their defences as their moats
solidified and brigands advanced over dry land. But the
Channel remained open, and across this Jean returned to England, honourably re-entering captivity. Jean the Goodnatured,
as they had nicknamed him, shared with the Prince of Wales
a respect for the ideals of an earlier generation. He was profoundly scandalized that his own son Louis should so basely
and publicly brand himself as 'forsworn and convicted of a
breach of honour'. He saw that only his own return could save
the family name. And by appointing his son Charles as regent
he was leaving France in more cunning hands.

His second period of captivity was brief. Shortly after Easter
1364 he died at the Palace of Savoy. Edward ordered court
mourning and attended a 'noble, magnificent and costly'
memorial service at St Paul's to which, loyal to his renunciation
of his claim to the throne of France, he had the dead king's
body borne in a cortège with 'the horses housed from head to
foot in the arms and lilies of France, the riders appropriately
and sumptuously adorned with the same emblems'. The corpse
lay in state, surrounded by 'eighty great candles, each twelve
feet high . . ., and four thousand wax tapers, each weighing six
pounds', before being returned to France for burial at Saint-
Denis.

Jean had died in his forty-fifth year, a man of high principles,
short-temper and bad judgement, an unsuccessful king. His son,
the regent Charles, learned of his death on 17 April 1364.

Within a month the new king had established himself with a small but significant victory.

Charles's brother-in-law, Carlos, who held several important castles and estates in Normandy, had been on bad terms with the French royal family since his accession to the throne of the small Pyrenean kingdom of Navarre in 1350. King Jean, whose daughter Carlos married in 1352, put him in prison in 1356 for plotting against him. Escaping from his fortress gaol after Poitiers, the King of Navarre accepted the title of Captain-General of Paris during the revolt against the regent led by Etienne Marcel and, though he later was nominally reconciled with Charles, he continued to intrigue with the English. A small, passionate, intelligent man, he was entirely untrust-

King Jean returns to London and captivity in place of his oathbreaking son Louis in January 1364.

worthy but cultivated by Edward and the Prince of Wales because he could be very useful to them and harmful to Charles. Shortly before Jean's death the prince had encouraged the Captal de Buch to accept the post of lieutenant to Carlos. The Captal was joined by the freelance company led by the famous English adventurer John Jewel.

To deal with the threat from Navarre's mercenaries, the new King Charles V sent to Normandy a band of his own, commanded by the guerrilla leader Bertrand de Claquin, better known as Duguesclin. Duguesclin, the swarthy, snub-nosed, squat son of a minor Breton noble family, was so ugly and unmannered that his parents had refused to allow him, even when a child, to sit at the same table as his nine brothers and sisters.

After aiding the abortive revolt of the merchants of Paris under Etienne Marcel, Carlos of Navarre (*left*) makes peace with his brother-in-law the Regent Dauphin Charles.

He had, not unnaturally, grown up to be an aggressive and resourceful fighter. His troops were largely Breton mercenaries whose record of atrocities had made them more feared by the French than any other brigands. The opposing forces, less than 2,000 men on each side, met on 16 May 1364 at the village of Cocherel, above the river Eure, midway between Evreux and Vernon. The Navarrese were convincingly defeated. Jewel was mortally wounded and the Captal taken prisoner.

There was great rejoicing in France, where the victory was seen as a triumph over 'the English', and as marking the turn of the tide in the nation's military fortunes. The Prince of Wales realized this, and sent Sir John Chandos into Brittany to continue the war by proxy against France. Although under the Treaty of Brétigny it had been agreed that the duchy of Brittany was a fief of France and the two rival dukes had sworn a truce before the prince and agreed to have their claims decided by arbitration, Charles of Blois had refused to cease fighting and Jean de Montfort struck back with enthusiasm. In July Montfort besieged the town and castle of Auray. Blois set off to its relief with an army of three or four thousand men, including a contingent headed by Duguesclin, who – like Chandos – was nominally acting in a private capacity. Both sides had some

*Opposite* Charles V of France.

150

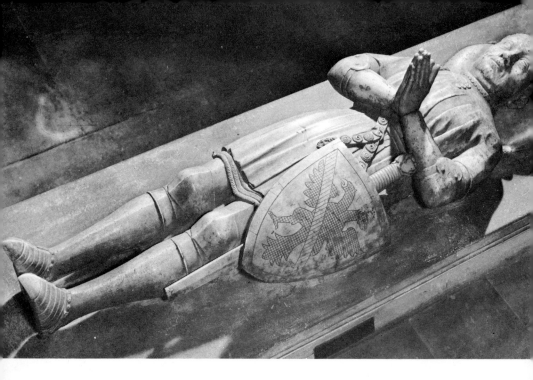

Breton troops. Montfort had men from famous Free Companies headed by Robert Knollys and Hugh Calveley but his total strength was probably one thousand less than that of Blois, who arrived at Auray on Sunday 29 September 1364. The battle that day was really a contest between Chandos and Duguesclin. Blois was killed, Duguesclin captured. The reputation of English arms was restored. Montfort met no further resistance and for the first time for twenty-three years Brittany was at peace under one unchallenged ruler.

Early in July 1364 the prince received a report from an English spy in Navarre, who, after begging that the letter should be burned (it was not, and is today in the British Museum) and its contents divulged to nobody, continued: 'know for certain that on Friday 21 June, the Count of Foix came to Saint-Palay [on the Bidouze, where Navarre meets Béarn] to speak with the King of Navarre and, in an avenue by the river they spoke of high matters entirely alone, and I was in another avenue of an adjoining house and heard every word.' The count (who held some of his lands as vassal of the prince) had received a visit from 'Maître Gontier, secrétaire du Roi de France' (Gontier de Baigneux, who carried out several confidential missions for members of the royal family),

Sir Robert Knollys, one of the most famous and successful of the Captains of Free Companies.

who had offered him the lieutenancy of Languedoc. He had accepted, and 'intended to hand over to his son Gaston the lands that he holds of the Prince, for he no longer wishes to be his man'. Gontier told him that 'the King of France was allied with the Count of Flanders ... and was negotiating alliances with the Count of Savoy and many other lords, and that he had sent to Scotland, and to another King whose name I have forgotten, to ask for help by sea'.

It was Charles's intention, said Gontier, 'to give a good reply in words to the English until he has recovered the hostages that are in England', but as soon as that was done he would 'make war on all sides against the English and the Principality, for ... King Charles will be Emperor and recover what has been lost to the English and in the end destroy them'. Meanwhile Charles proposed to make war on the King of Navarre in Normandy and Montfort in Brittany and under cover of these operations continue to recruit men-at-arms. His envoys were at Harfleur ready to go by sea to the King of Castile. He asked Foix not to release the Count of Armagnac (who had attacked him and been captured in December 1362): 'he is too artful and, if free, would soon come to an agreement with the Prince.' Foix also said that he would readily act as mediator between

153

The letter from an English spy to the Prince of Wales, warning him of the negotiations of Gontier de Baigneux.

Carlos of Navarre and Charles of France so that they could all three join forces against the English.

A little earlier, while the prince was inspecting fortresses in the county of Bigorre, surrendered under the Treaty of Brétigny, the Count of Foix had ridden over to Tarbes from Pau to pay his respects. Armagnac, who was also present, asked the prince to use his influence with Foix to have his (Armagnac's) ransom of 250,000 francs remitted or reduced. The prince would have none of it, and told Armagnac that he had been captured in fair fight after having 'put my cousin the Earl of Foix in adventure against you', and that Foix was entitled to his reward, adding that in similar circumstances 'my lord my father and I would not be content that we should be desired to leave what we have won by good adventure'.

Armagnac then addressed himself to the princess, knowing the difficulty she always had in refusing a favour. She agreed to help and asked Foix if he would make her a present. Guessing what she had in mind, he replied that he was a poor knight, all of whose money was needed for keeping his towns and fortresses in repair, but 'if the thing that ye desire pass not the value of threescore thousand francs, I will give it to you gladly'. Exercising all her great charm, she pressed him to promise that he would grant what she asked. He repeated that he could not afford any gift worth more than 60,000 francs. She continued: 'Gentle Earl of Foix, the request that I desire of you is to forgive entirely the Earl of Armagnac.' Foix refused to remit the whole ransom but agreed that it should be reduced, by the 60,000 francs he had promised her, to 190,000 francs.

The prince later lent Armagnac money and persuaded others of his vassals to make up the rest of the debt so that he could be free. Armagnac's gratitude to his two principal benefactors did not prove to be long-lasting.

But these were only small straws in the wind. The intelligent Charles, patient, efficient and vengeful where his father had been stupid and rash, was determined to regain all that King Jean had lost – and more. He was already deep in secret negotiations that would lead to a resumption of the war against the English on an entirely new front.

Chapter Seven

# The Spanish Adventure

During the three and a quarter centuries since the Moorish tide of invasion began to ebb from Spain, the ancient kingdom of the Visigoths had split into five parts: Portugal, Castile, Navarre, Aragon and Granada. Castile, by far the largest, extended from the Atlantic coasts of Galicia and Asturias in the north-west down to Andalucia, on the Atlantic again in the south-west, and Murcia on the Mediterranean. It was the only kingdom which had a common frontier with the infidel-infested Granada which stretched in a narrow crescent from the Strait of Gibraltar to the Gulf of Mazarron. From the Castilian border near Alicante northward to the Pyrenees at the Pic d'Anie, and up the Mediterranean coast beyond Perpignan, the kingdom of Aragon took in Valencia, Catalonia and the county of Roussillon. North of Castile, between Aragon and the Bay of Biscay, the comparatively tiny kingdom of Navarre straddled the Pyrenees from Saint-Jean-Pied-de-Port to Tudela.

The energetic, brazen and inventively perfidious King of Navarre, Carlos (nicknamed the Bad because of his uncertain and violent temper), had played a prominent and meddlesome part in Anglo-French relations since he succeeded to his throne in 1350 at the age of eighteen. His brother-in-law, Peter of Aragon (nicknamed the Ceremonious because of his punctilious concern for etiquette), had since 1356 been a close ally of France, to whom he supplied galleys for use against the English, and was the active supporter of Henry of Trastamara (nicknamed the Bastard because he was one) in Henry's attempt to usurp the throne of Castile. This throne was occupied by Pedro I, who was nicknamed the Cruel, not because he was noticeably more or less inhuman than his Bad, Ceremonious or Bastard contemporaries (Peter for instance personally designed the cage in which he kept a nephew locked up for four years, and punished a group of rebels by making them drink the molten metal of bells they had rung to signal their revolt) but because he had been 'rude and rebel against the commandments of Holy Church' and was therefore unremittingly denigrated by every monkish chronicler in Christendom.

Pedro was the only son born in wedlock to Alfonso XI of Castile, who had ten illegitimate children by a mistress named Leonor de Guzman. The eldest of these, Henry Count of Trastamara, was Pedro's senior by one year. Pedro would have become the Prince of Wales's brother-in-law had not his fiancée, the prince's sister Joanna of the Tower, died of the plague on her way to her wedding at Burgos in 1348. And Henry might well have become one of the prince's closest companions, for Edward III had offered to bring up one of Doña Leonor's sons with his own in 1345, when Henry was twelve and the prince fifteen.

The interest of the English royal family in that of Castile stemmed from their importance as naval allies. On land the warriors of the peninsula were still, even in the 1360s, cavorting about in chain armour that provided little protection against the longbow, accompanied by hordes of ill-armed peons to serve as buffers against the enemy cavalry. But the Castilians were formidable at sea, where their great thirty-bench galleys, built specially for war, were vastly more effective and manoeuvrable than the square-rigged, single-masted merchant vessels that the English and French pressed into service when needed. There had long been commercial contact between England and Castile – Spanish wines were credited in England with having greater strength than Gascon claret; Santiago de Compostela was a particular favourite with English pilgrims; English knights, including the Earl of Derby, the Princess of Wales's former husband Thomas Holland, and one of her fathers-in-law, Salisbury, had served in Alfonso XI's crusade against the Moors on his southern border. But Castile's need to keep an ally on the far side of Aragon, and the influence of a succession of French popes, induced Alfonso XI to sign an alliance with Philippe of France in 1345.

Pedro the Cruel:
the head is
contemporary but
the nose has been
restored.

Pedro succeeded Alfonso in 1350 at the age of sixteen. He was tall, well-built, blue-eyed and fair-haired, with a dominating nose and great vitality. In 1354 some of his leading vassals tried to depose him in favour of his half-brother Henry of Trastamara, but Pedro quelled the revolt with the help of the loyal middle classes. From 1356 he waged an inconclusive war against Henry's backer, Peter of Aragon, and in 1362 entered into a formal alliance with England. In the spring of 1363 he forced Peter to accept a peace treaty and to surrender territory on his western border.

The terms were of no great significance, for neither ruler intended to abide by them. Peter of Aragon, finding great opposition to the treaty among his own subjects, refused to ratify it and had his principal adviser publicly beheaded as a scapegoat. He then joined with Henry of Trastamara to buy Carlos of Navarre's support with the promise of a share of Castilian territory. So the war between Castile and Aragon, which had seemed at an end when the Prince of Wales arrived to take possession of Aquitaine in the summer of 1363, was in full flame again by the time that the mayor and aldermen of London on the last day of March 1365 received a letter from 'the Princess of Gascony and Wales: "Be pleased to know that on Monday the 27th day of January, we were delivered of a son, with safety to ourselves and to the infant, for the which may God be thanked for His Might; and may he always have you in his keeping. Given under our seal, at the Castle of Engosleme, the 4th day of February."' The boy was the prince's first legitimate child, the princess's sixth. He was christened Edward in the cathedral of Saint-Pierre at Angoulême by Jean de Cros, Bishop of Limoges.

The birth of this child, second in line to the throne, was one of the few occasions for rejoicing in a sombre year. In England there was a 'great abundance of rain and hay was lost. There was so much fighting amongst sparrows in that season, that they were found dead on the ground in great numbers. Also there followed great mortality of people, the sickness being so sharp and vehement, that many being in perfect health one night when they went to bed were found dead in the morning. Also many died of the small pocks, both men, women and children.' Abroad it was clear that the new King of France was preparing to denounce the treaties of Brétigny and Calais and launch attacks from every quarter.

From his spies the prince learned that Charles V had sent his confidential agent Gontier to Peter of Aragon to propose a secret alliance with the object of invading Navarre. The trickery had become so complicated that Charles was simultaneously proposing to Carlos of Navarre a treaty of peace; to Peter of Aragon war against Navarre; and to the pope a revival of the plan to send the Free Companies into Castile to put Henry of Trastamara on Pedro's throne; while in Toulouse, Charles's brother Louis of Anjou, lieutenant-general in Languedoc, was discussing with the Aragonese emissaries to the pope a plan to divert the companies to an attack on Navarre followed by a combined assault on Aquitaine.

Information on the full extent of Charles's plans probably did not reach the prince until the late summer, for in May 1365 he seems to have complied with Pope Urban's request to give aid to Duguesclin, who was, His Holiness alleged, passing through Gascony on his way to crusade against the Moors of Granada. Duguesclin's true mission was to lead the companies first against Castile, then against Navarre, then against Aquitaine. The wages for himself, his second-in-command the French Marshal Audrehem, and the men of the companies, were to be paid in equal thirds by Charles V, Peter of Aragon, and the pope. Apart from Duguesclin's much feared Bretons and the privately engaged French under Audrehem, the largest of the companies was that led by the Englishman, Sir Hugh Calveley, who had played a leading part in Duguesclin's defeat at Auray. Before the end of the year they began crossing into Catalonia. Peter sent officers to direct them through to Castile and gave instructions that all women, children, movable property and provisions should be brought in from the villages to the towns for protection until these locusts had passed on their way to Saragossa. Not all the precautions were successful. On Candlemas Day, 2 February 1366, two hundred inhabitants of Barbastro who had taken refuge in the church tower were burned alive by mercenaries in the temporary service of their king.

In the early days of March 1366 the men of the companies struck up the Ebro almost to Logroño and then westward past

Nájera to Burgos where, on Palm Sunday, 29 March, Henry
of Trastamara was proclaimed king. His troops, justifying the
claim that they were on a crusade, slaughtered many Saracens
and a few Jews whom they hunted out of the city, reserving
the richer Jews to be squeezed for money for their next instalment of wages. There was little serious resistance. Though
the middle classes still favoured Pedro, the magnates were more
than ever eager to welcome a new and possibly less severe
master.

Pedro, who left Burgos only a day before Henry entered, rode
with a small escort to Toledo, and from there to Seville. But
Seville turned against him. He fled back towards the Tagus,
intending to take refuge with his uncle, Pedro the Severe, King
of Portugal. At Albuquerque the commander of his own garrison refused him entrance. In Portugal the royal council denied
him sanctuary. He continued northwards, out over the Portu-
guese frontier and into the province of Galicia, whose governor
had remained loyal to him. At Corunna he was met by a messenger from the Prince of Wales – Lord Poynings, who brought
him the prince's assurance that he would do everything possible
to restore him to the throne of Castile. Pedro set sail for Bayonne
to confer with this friend in need. Sir Thomas Felton, Seneschal
of Aquitaine, was waiting to escort him from Bayonne to Bordeaux, where they arrived at the beginning of July 1366. Outside Bordeaux he was received with great respect and ceremony
by the prince, who insisted that the royal refugee should lead
the procession into the city.

The prince was ready to support Pedro for several reasons.
Strategically he wished to have a friendly power on his southern
flank, and the support of Castilian galleys on the high seas. On
moral grounds (a consideration that did not weigh heavily with
most of his royal contemporaries) he was bound by the terms
of the Anglo-Castilian treaty of 1362, despite the scandalous
propaganda so diligently spread by Pedro's enemies: 'a change-
ling ...; a child of Jewish parentage whom the Queen secretly
substituted for the girl to whom she had just given birth ...
a man of evil and disgraceful life,' said Venette; 'a lover of Jews
and Pagans more than Christians,' said another monkish
chronicler; 'a bugger and unbeliever,' said the pope. By personal preference he welcomed the chance of adventure, for 'in

161

this season the Prince was in the lusty flower of youth, and he was never weary nor full satisfied of war, since the first beginning that he bore arms, but ever intended to achieve high deeds'. Finally, on a point of principle that touched him closely, when his council advised him not to give aid to a man 'right cruel and full of evil conditions ..., enemy to the Church and cursed by our Holy Father the Pope', the prince replied that 'It is not convenable that a bastard should hold a realm in heritage, and put out of his own realm his brother, rightful inheritor to the land; the which thing all Kings and Kings's sons should in no wise suffer or consent to, for it is a great prejudice against the state royal.'

It was not the prince's responsibility to bear the costs of what would be a very expensive expedition; but Pedro had arrived with comparatively little in his pockets. He saved his extensive personal collection of jewellery, but the galley bearing most of his treasure was treacherously surrendered to Henry of Trastamara. He promised to reimburse the prince and to give him the whole of the province of Viscaya, which included the important city and port of Bilbao, if he would advance the initial funds for the expedition. The amount required was considerable, for payment had to be made not only to the Anglo-Gascon army that the prince undertook to assemble, but also to Carlos the Bad in his capacity as 'Gatekeeper of the Pyrenees'.

Carlos's Navarre was completely enclosed by Aquitaine, France, Aragon and Castile. Nature had bountifully equipped him with the talent for double-dealing that was demanded by the geographical location of his kingdom. In May 1362 he signed an alliance with Pedro of Castile; in the autumn of 1363 he deserted Pedro for Peter of Aragon. In the autumn of 1365 he was back with Pedro; in December with Peter again. Now, in July 1366, he came to Bordeaux to discuss a new alliance with Pedro.

There was at that time no practicable road from Bayonne to San Sebastian along the coast. The only route for an army from Aquitaine into Spain ran from Saint-Jean-Pied-de-Port up to the pass of Roncesvalles, where Roland had slain 100,000 Saracens and died six centuries before, and down to Pamplona. It was the road taken by most of the foot pilgrims to the shrine of St James at Compostela (the English often preferred to go

Carlos of Navarre,
from a window in
the Cathedral at
Evreux.

163

by sea down through the Bay of Biscay) and the whole of its length was within Navarrese territory. Carlos had probably already decided that he could not refuse a request to open the pass if it came from so powerful a figure as the Prince of Wales, but he meant to make Pedro pay well for the privilege of using it. He did. The terms finally agreed in the treaty signed at Libourne on 23 September by the three leaders provided for the cession by Pedro to Carlos of the entire province of Guipuz-coa, which separated Navarre from the Atlantic, the neigh-bouring province of Alava, and all the fortresses on the Castilian bank of the Ebro from Haro down to Alfaro. Carlos was to be paid 200,000 florins because of the risks he was taking in siding with Pedro, and 36,000 florins a month for the 1,000 mounted men and 1,000 foot that he would contribute to the allied army.

The Prince of Wales's own army was expected to cost 250,000 florins over six months, and the contingents under individual Gascon lords another 300,000 for the same period. The prince undertook to pay these and the amounts promised to Navarre until 10 January 1367 – the money to be repaid to him when Pedro regained his kingdom. Meanwhile, the prince gave orders for his household gold and silver to be melted down and minted into coins and for the English and Gascon mercenary companies to be summoned back from Spain before they found themselves fighting against their own prince.

In England the king and his council had agreed that, to avoid an open split with France, the invasion should be conducted by the prince solely in his capacity as overlord of Aquitaine, though John of Gaunt, who had succeeded to the title of Lan-caster when his father-in-law died in 1362, was permitted to lend his brother support with 400 men-at-arms and 800 archers. For similar reasons, Charles V pretended ignorance of the agreement which his brother Louis signed with Peter of Aragon to make a simultaneous attack on Navarre from north and south of the Pyrenees. Carlos, however, got wind of these negotiations. He consequently approached Henry of Trastamara in January 1367 and struck a bargain to keep the pass of Roncesvalles closed in return for the surrender of Logroño and 60,000 Castilian gold doubloons, each worth approximately three-quarters of a florin. Convinced that Carlos had exhausted all the possible permutations of betrayal, Peter of Aragon wrote to the governor of his province of Roussillon on 25 January 1367, assuring him that the Prince of Wales's expedition had been cancelled because of Carlos's defection.

He was wrong on both counts. The prince had remained in Bordeaux during the early days of January to await the birth of his second child – a boy whom he named Richard. Joan was heartbroken to see him go. 'She reproached the Goddess of Love who had brought her to such high majesty, for she had the most puissant Prince who lived in this age. Often she said, "Alas, what should I do . . . if I were to lose the very flower of nobility, the flower of highest grandeur, of whom the world can name no peer for valour . . .? For all the world says this, that never did any man embark on so perilous an expedition."' The prince 'gently comforted the lady, and then sweetly took leave of her, saying lovingly: "Lady, we shall meet again in joyous fashion, we and all our friends, for so my heart tells me."' He moved down to Dax, where his army was assembled, on the 10th and was joined there on the 13th by his brother John, who had brought his contingent of 1,200 men over to Brittany and down through Poitou.

Not all the men the prince had summoned were present. And some who had come were none too happy. Arnaud d'Albret, for instance, who was a nephew of the Count of Armagnac, had offered to provide 1,000 men; the prince said he would need (and possibly could afford to pay) only 200. Albret protested that he had already engaged 1,000 and, if he had to discharge one, he would discharge them all. The prince angrily exclaimed, 'The Sire d'Albret is a great lord indeed when he wishes to break the ordinance of my Council. By God, things shall not be as he thinks. Let him stay at home if he likes: I can do without his 1,000 lances.' D'Albret joined the expedition, but never forgave him. Another ally of doubtful loyalty – Gaston of Foix – had excused himself from coming to the conference with Pedro at Libourne 'because he had a disease in his leg and might not ride', evidently not wishing to commit himself until he had held discussion with the French. He refused permission for the English mercenaries to cross his borders on their return from Spain. When he arrived at Dax just before the expedition moved off and offered his services, the prince

Two presumed portraits of Joan of Kent: *right*, on a boss in the chantry which her husband the Prince of Wales endowed in Canterbury Cathedral; *opposite*, taken from a stone figure (from Francis Peck's *History of Stamford*, 1727).

politely asked him to go back and protect his own country – probably fearing treachery if he came with him.

On hearing of Carlos's betrayal, the prince had sent an order to Sir Hugh Calveley to invade Navarre. Calveley had remained in the service of Henry of Trastamara when the other English and Gascon mercenaries quit. It was quite possibly on the prince's orders that he did so, for he was now on the border of Castile and Navarre, at Calahorra, admirably placed to join the prince when he came over the Pyrenees or – as he did now – to ride up the river Arga towards Pamplona, capturing the Navarrese fortresses of Miranda and Puente la Reina as he went. Carlos took the hint: when the prince reached Peyre-horade in the foothills of the Pyrenees the King of Navarre was waiting for him there: to assure him that the pass of Roncesvalles was open as agreed. The army moved across the frontier into Navarre and gathered round the town of Saint-Jean at the foot of the pass.

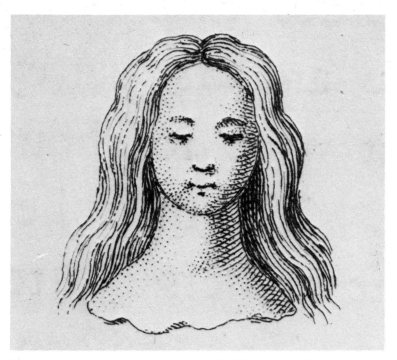

There were perhaps as many as 10,000 men and perhaps as few as 4,000 in the prince's army which began the sixteen mile climb to Roncesvalles, 3,500 feet above sea level, about 14 February 1367. The winter was at its worst. 'Since the just God suffered death for us on the Cross,' wrote the herald of Sir John Chandos who was with the vanguard, 'there was never so difficult a passage, for one saw men and horses, that suffered many ills, stumble through the mountain; for there was no comradeship; the father did not tarry for the son; there was cold so great, snow and frost also, that each one was dismayed.' After breaking their journey at the great fortified monastery at the top of the pass they descended to Burguete and Pamplona.

News of the threatened invasion reached Burgos about 24 February. The problem of finding money to retain large bodies of troops – which was one of the factors that prompted the Prince of Wales to press on with the campaign despite the bitter weather – had forced Henry of Trastamara to discharge most of his foreign mercenaries despite increasing unrest among his subjects, many of whom, oppressed by new taxes, now wished

Pedro to return. Henry despatched messengers to urge Duguesclin to retrace his steps (his company was making its unwelcome
way through Aragon back to France) and himself moved to
Santo Domingo de la Calzada, halfway between Burgos and
Logroño, where he ordered his army to join him.

From Pamplona two roads lead to Burgos: the southerly by
way of Logroño (the modern N.121, N.111, and N.120) and
the northerly through Vitoria and Miranda de Ebro (N.240,
N.1). The prince sent a detachment of between four and five
hundred men-at-arms and mounted archers down the southerly
road, commanded by Sir William Felton. At Logroño, which
was still held by Pedro's supporters, they crossed the swollen,
fast-flowing Ebro, pressed on to Navarrete and shortly afterwards sent back word to the prince that they were in contact
with Henry's outposts. The prince was advancing along the
upper road towards Vitoria. His intention was evidently to take
Henry in a pincer movement, and at the same time to avoid
being attacked on two sides by Henry and Peter of Aragon as
he might have been had he committed the whole of his force
to the Logroño road. But without a map and, despite Pedro's
presence, badly advised on local conditions, he soon found that
he had embarked on a second appalling winter journey through
hill country where food was scarce for both men and horses. At
Salvatierra, some fifteen miles short of Vitoria, he halted so that
they could rest and collect provisions. It was probably here that
he received a letter: 'Henry, by the Grace of God, King of Castile, of Leon, of Toledo, of Galicia, of Sevile, of Cordoba, of
Murcia, of Jaën, of Algarve, of Algeciras, and Lord of Molina.
To the most puissant Prince Edward, Prince of Aquitaine and
Wales, greetings! We have heard that you would enter our
Kingdom of Castile in great force, with our enemy and adver-
sary, at which we marvel, for we do not believe we have any
quarrel with you . . . We therefore send to you to know at which
place you intend to enter our aforesaid Kingdom of Castile,
for with the aid of God and our good subjects and friends we
shall come to meet you, and it will not be long before you shall
have battle, for it is also reported to us that you and your gentry
much desire it. We wish that God, you and all the world shall
know that this is not our desire, but we are of necessity obliged
and constrained to defend our realm and our subjects.'

168

The letter was written at Santo Domingo on 28 February. Henry's army was still assembling in the shelter of the nearby cork oak forests at Bañares. When Duguesclin and the Marshal Audrehem joined him, returning from Aragon with their Breton and French companies, they warned Henry not to risk a pitched battle with so daunting an opponent as the prince. This advice was supported by Charles of France, who wrote urging Trastamara to adopt his own tactics of passive resistance: retire to a strong position, harass the flanks of the invaders, and allow them to exhaust themselves in despoiling the rest of the country. But Henry was well aware that the Castilian malcontents were as ready to desert him as they had recently been to desert Pedro. And once he began to retreat he would meet the same fate as Pedro. Accordingly he moved north to confront the Prince of Wales. Felton, to the east, kept a day's march ahead, maintaining station between the two armies and sending reports to the prince. 'And when the Prince heard the matter ..., how the Bastard was coming straight to him, desiring battle, then he said: "So help me, Jesus Christ, right hardy is this Bastard. In God's name let us go to meet him, my lords, and take up our position before Vitoria."'

While the troops were arrayed outside the city by the two marshals, the prince, his brother the Duke of Lancaster, and other leaders 'made that day more than two hundred knights', including one of the prince's stepsons, Thomas Holland. The ceremony implied more than the conferring of honour. To the serving squire in the field the tap on the shoulder and the words 'Be thou a Knight' meant the authority to command, a rise in wages, and the likelihood that if he was wounded his captors would consider it worth while preserving him for ransom rather than slitting his throat. But the new knights were not to be put to the test immediately. 'All day they were arrayed in battle-order and ready for the onset ... At vespers they went to their quarters. Then the Prince had it cried about that each one should return the next day right to that plain ..., and round about there was no hovel nor house that was not full of his men.'

Felton established his detachment at Ariñez, about five miles to the west. Ahead of him, in the mountains that blocked the way to Miranda and the crossing of the Ebro, Henry had halted at Anastro and sent his vanguard to the fortress of Zaldiaran: virtually impregnable, set on a peak above a river gorge, dominating the road to Miranda and commanding a view over the Vitoria plain. That night Henry sent his brother, Don Tello, with a large force of French men-at-arms and Castilian light horsemen, to hunt down the enemy foraging parties and outposts. They surprised Hugh Calveley at dawn, preparing to saddle up and return to Vitoria. The Castilians 'did much damage to his sumpter beasts and waggons, whereupon noise and cries arose, and the currours ran up and down through the camp: many were killed in their beds'.

The alarm roused the Duke of Lancaster, who brought elements of the vanguard to the rescue. Don Tello withdrew, but did not return directly to Zaldiaran. Sweeping the countryside for further prey, he came upon Felton. Heavily outnumbered – Chandos Herald says the odds were sixty to one – the English retired to a hill from which their archers managed for some time to keep the Castilians at bay. 'Sir William the valiant, right hardy and courageous, charged with lance in rest among the enemy like a man devoid of sense and discretion ... Striking a Spaniard upon his flowered shield', he thrust his lance through his opponent's armour and into his heart, then drew his sword and attacked the others who 'followed him on every side and threw spears and darts at him' until they brought him down and killed him. His companions continued to fight off these spear-throwing *jinetes* with archery and lance-charges on foot until the attackers were reinforced by Audrehem's heavily armoured men-at-arms. These, also dismounting, overwhelmed the defenders by sheer weight of numbers. The bravery of Felton and his men so impressed observers that the place was renamed – and remained – *Inglesmondi*, the Hill of the Englishmen, 'where they twanged the yew and raised the battle-axe, and left behind them a name of glory at Inglis Mendi, a name that shall last until fire consumes the Cantabrian hills', as George Borrow wrote when the spot was pointed out to him nearly five hundred years later.

By this time the main English forces were standing to, prepared for a decisive battle. The prince 'thought certainly that all the enemy's army had come down through the pass'. He waited all day but the expected attack never came. Henry had

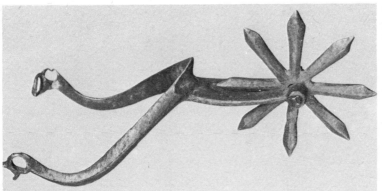

An eight-rowelled
spur used in the
second half of the
fourteenth century.

accepted the French plan. In the days that followed, the Castilians continued their hit-and-run raids, and the prince's men suffered further hardships: 'In the Prince's host a loaf of bread was
sold for a florin, every man glad to give, and more an they could
have got it.' On Monday 29 March 1367 he broke camp. It was
clear that Henry would not come into the open, and that the
road to Miranda could not be forced. They must continue the
advance on Burgos by another route. He led his men south-
east over the mountains, meeting the Pamplona – Logroño road
at Viana just short of the left bank of the Ebro. By Wednesday
he had most of his men across the river and 'camped that day
before Logroño in the orchards and under the olive trees'.

Henry, on hearing of the prince's moves, marched his army
rapidly back to his starting point at Santo Domingo and then
forward to Nájera. It was there, on 1 April, that the prince sent
back the herald who had brought Henry's letter more than a
month before: 'Edward, eldest son of the King of England,
Prince of Aquitaine and of Wales, Duke of Cornwall and Earl
of Chester. To the noble and puissant Henry, Count of Triste-
mary, greetings. We have received your letter in which you take
upon yourself the title of King of Castile ...' He affirmed his
intention, 'because of ancient and recent alliances made by the
predecessors of the King of Castile Don Pedro and by him on
the one hand and by the predecessors of our most dear lord
and father and by him and by us on the other hand, to aid
the said King Don Pedro in his prerogative and rights'. But
because 'we would that God, you and all men shall know that
we desire neither battle nor the shedding of blood between

Christians, if such may be avoided without injury to our honour and the heritage of ourselves and our friends and allies', he promised that if Henry would surrender the kingdom he would guarantee the usurper and his supporters a free pardon and would see that any grievances they had against Don Pedro were settled to their satisfaction.

Henry sent back a reply which did not conceal his irritation at the prince's form of address: 'Henry, by the Grace of God King of Castile and of Leon, of Toledo, of Galicia, of Sevile and of Cordoba, of Algarve and of Algeciras and Lord of Molina. To you, Edward Prince of Wales, calling yourself eldest son of the King of England and Prince of Aquitaine, greetings ...' He remarked that 'it seems to some, indeed to many, that you are much preoccupied with vain glory'. He suggested that two or three knights from each side should meet to agree upon a site for the battle.

The prince, still acutely short of supplies, was not inclined to waste any more time. On 2 April he moved forward to Navarrete, the town which Felton had reached during his reconnaissance. That afternoon his scouts brought word that Henry's army had advanced from Nájera across the Najerilla – a river subject to flash-flooding in the spring – and was being marshalled about two miles to the east along a tributary whose steep banks provided an obstacle to anybody attacking along the Navarrete–Nájera road. Though they did not take up their final positions until midnight, the general disposition of Henry's forces was clear: the van, commanded by Duguesclin, was composed of dismounted French mercenaries and the scarlet-sashed knights of the Orden de la Banda, an order of chivalry founded by Alfonso XI. Behind them stood the principal 'battle' of Castilian and Aragonese men-at-arms, *jinetes* and infantry under the command of King Henry. On each flank were detachments of cavalry under Henry's brother Don Tello and the Count of Denia, a cousin of Peter of Aragon.

Some seven or eight miles away at Navarrete 'in the evening the Prince caused secretly to be shewed through all the host that at the first sowning of the trumpets every man to apparel himself, and at the second to be armed, and at the third to leap a-horseback and to follow the marshals' banners with the pennon of St George'. It was before first light that the trumpets sounded, for the prince had no intention of letting Henry fight on ground of his own choice. To the right of the Navarrete–Nájera road rose the hill of Cuento, a high ridge which completely concealed the prince's army as, swinging off the direct road, he made a detour to the north and, at dawn, suddenly appeared on Henry's left flank.

While Duguesclin hurriedly attempted to remarshal the vanguard to face this unexpected angle of attack, the prince ordered his men to dismount and swiftly harangued them. '"Sirs! You know well that we are nearly overtaken by famine, and you see there our enemies who have plenty of victuals, bread and wine, and fish both salt and fresh. But we must conquer them by stroke of lance and sword. Now let us act this day that we may depart in honour." Then the valiant Prince clasped his hands to heaven and said: "True sovereign Father, who has made and created us, as truly as Thou dost know that I am not come here except to uphold the right, and for prowess and nobility which prompt my heart to gain a life of honour, I beseech Thee that Thou wilt this day guard me and my men." And when the Prince, graceful to look upon, had made his prayer to God, then he said, "Forward, Banner! God help us to our right!"'

The vanguard under Lancaster and Chandos advanced against Duguesclin's men. Behind them was the prince's main division, with the Captal de Buch's Gascons on his right and English cavalry on his left. The rearguard was posted on the slope of the hilly ground that had masked the prince's approach: a medley from many quarters, their leaders including Hugh Calveley, James of Majorca, whose kingdom had been seized by Peter of Aragon, and the Count of Armagnac.

One figure was noticeably missing – the dark, small, clever King of Navarre. When he learned that the Prince of Wales was halted and possibly stalemated outside Vitoria, Carlos made a swift reassessment of his position. If the prince gave up his attempt to replace Pedro on the throne of Castile, Henry of Trastamara and Peter of Aragon would take revenge on Carlos for having let the prince through the Pass of Ronces-

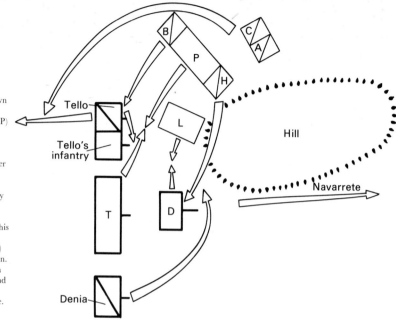

Trastamara (T) with Duguesclin (D) as vanguard, awaits attack down Navarrete road. Prince of Wales (P) appears from behind hill on North East, launches Lancaster (L) against Duguesclin, his right flank cavalry under Captal de Buch (B) against Tello, who flees, his left flank cavalry under Hewitt (H) against Duguesclin. Tello sends Denia against Hewitt and himself advances against the prince. Hewitt smashes Denia. Prince defeats Trastamara. Calveley and Armagnac pursue.

## THE BATTLE OF NÁJERA, SATURDAY 3 APRIL 1367

valles. On the other hand, if the prince, a stubborn and renowned warrior, overcame the obstacles that confronted him, neither he nor Don Pedro was likely to forgive Carlos for any help he might give to Henry or Peter in the hope of hedging his bets. It was a moment when any course of action was fraught with the possibility of evil consequences. Carlos wisely decided to put himself in a position where no action could be taken. He had himself 'taken prisoner' by Duguesclin's cousin, Olivier de Mauny, who had been left in command of a fortress on the border of Aragon and Navarre. 'The Prince and all his party had great marvel,' as Froissart noted, 'and some in the Prince's host supposed it was done by a cautel by his own means ...,' because he knew not how the matter should go between King Henry and King Don Pedro.' However, the prince with his usual gallantry assured the sorrowing Queen of Navarre that 'this our viage once achieved, we shall intend to no other thing but for his deliverance'. It eventually turned out that as soon as the campaign was over the King of Navarre was released

174

as inexplicably as he had been captured – and promptly clapped his gaoler accomplice into prison so that Mauny was unable to give evidence about the existence of any 'cautel' or to claim the estates that Carlos was reputed to have promised him in Normandy.

Though Carlos was absent from the battle, his banner was carried there by his chamberlain, Martin Enriquez, at the head of three hundred Navarrese men-at-arms. The total numbers engaged on each side are unknown, but were probably about equal. They advanced towards each other 'on a fair and beautiful plain, where there was neither bush nor tree for a full league round, by a fine river very rapid and fierce ... Now commenced fierce battle, and the dust began to rise.' Duguesclin's men, heavily armoured and on foot, stood up well to the hail of arrows from the English longbows. His Spanish crossbowmen, their heavy bolts more effective at closer quarters, almost broke the English advance. But Lancaster and Chandos strode on at the head of their men-at-arms. 'Great was the noise and frenzy ... There was neither banner nor pennon that was not thrown to the ground' amid the clash of weapons and the shouts of 'Castile! Santiago!' 'Guienne! St George!' Chandos was knocked down by an enormous Spaniard who leaped on him and stabbed him through the vizor. Chandos drew his own dagger and plunged it into his opponent's side, killing him; then he 'leapt to his feet, and grasped his sword with both hands and plunged again into the mêlée, which was fierce and terrible and marvellous to behold'.

The English vanguard shuddered at this savage impact with Duguesclin's wall of flailing steel. As the prince brought the main division of his army down the slope, Trastamara ordered his brother Don Tello to attack Lancaster's right flank with his mixed force of light cavalry and infantrymen. The *jinetes* were trained to fight in the Moorish style, circling the enemy on their swift little horses, hurling darts and javelins. But neither speed nor their old-fashioned haubergeons and gambesons and narrow leather shields could protect them against the strength and accuracy of the English bowmen. They fled; and it was said that Don Tello was the first to run. The Captal de Buch's squadron, brought up by the Prince of Wales in reply, rode down Don Tello's unprotected Castilian infantry, slashing and thrust-

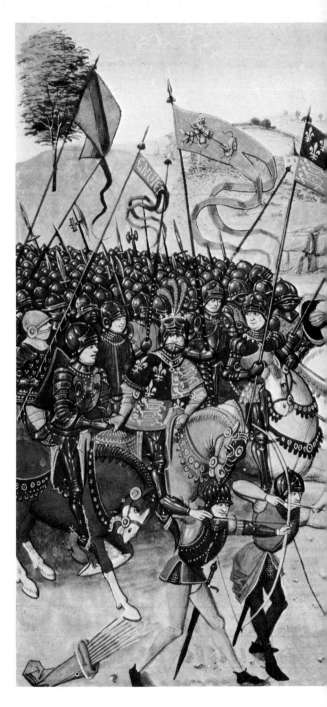

The Battle of
Nájera. The
illustrator, working
some years later,
wrongly shows the
Prince of Wales's
helmet crested with
ostrich feathers of
peace instead of his
lion of war.

ing. And now the prince called in the cavalry from his left wing. Hurling aside the efforts of the opposing Aragonese horsemen under the Count of Denia to stop them, they smashed into Duguesclin's right flank.

Trastamara's vanguard was now hemmed in on three sides. He rode forward at the head of his heavy cavalry, determined to thrust a way through and take the weight of the Prince of Wales's attack. But the Spanish horses were as inadequately protected as their riders. As they entered the barrage put down by the English bowmen they faltered and then turned away. Henry, a brave man in a desperate situation, galloped among them, shouting 'Lords, I am your King: ye have made me King of Castile, and have sworn and promised that to die ye will not fail me. For God's sake keep your promise that ye have sworn, and acquit you against me, and I shall acquit me against you; for I shall not fly one foot as long as I may see you do your devoir.'

Three times his main battle faltered and broke. Twice he cajoled and bullied them into returning. The third time they collapsed into uncontrolled flight, dragging the whole Castilian front into panic with them. The Prince of Wales sent his un-committed rearguard in pursuit of the fugitives who, finding the waters of the Najerilla tumultuous and swollen by a sudden spate, crowded in a hopeless jumble at the bridge to Nájera. 'There might you see knights leap into the water for fear, and die one upon the other, and it was said that by great marvel the river was red with the blood that flowed from the bodies of the dead men and horses.' Even for those who managed to force their way across the bridge, the town of Nájera was diffi-cult to escape from – the river in front, rugged cliffs at the rear. The Grand Master of the Order of Calatrava was found hiding in a cellar. The Prior of the Order of Santiago, another of the religious fellowships of chivalry born of the crusades against the Moors, was taken while trying to clamber over the town walls and almost killed out of hand before he could convince his cap-tors that he was able to pay a good ransom.

The triumphant Pedro, who had fought bravely in the prince's main battle, scoured the plain on his black charger, accompanied by his standard-bearer and shouting, 'Where is that whoreson that called himself King of Castile?' As he made his way back towards the prince's rallying point he came upon a Gascon knight leading a prisoner – Inigo Lopez Orozco, one of his former favourites who had gone over to Trastamara. Brushing aside the Gascon's protests, he killed Orozco on the spot. The action was as illegal as it was murderous, for before leaving Gascony he had accepted the Prince of Wales's stipulation that all prisoners should remain the property of those who captured them.

That night the prince enjoyed the victor's privilege of lodging in his enemy's tents – luxuriously supplied with 'wine and bread, coffers, vessels, gold and silver'. To Pedro, still vowing vengeance on his disloyal subjects, and pleading that those captured should be surrendered to him for execution, he said, '"Sir King, I beg you, grant me a gift, if it please you." Said Pedro: "Alas! Wherefore, Sire, do you ask me? All that I have is yours." Then the Prince said without delay: "Sire, I wish for naught of yours. But I counsel you for good, if you wish to be King of Castile, that you send news everywhere that you have granted this gift: to bestow pardon on all who have been against you . . ., provided that of their own free will they come to pray you mercy."' Pedro agreed.

The battle had ended at noon. By nightfall the four knights and four heralds who had been sent to identify the notable dead returned to make their report to the prince. 'The Bastard – is he dead or captured?' he asked. They replied that there was no trace of him. 'Then,' said the prince, 'we have done nothing.'

'Dearest and only sweetheart, well-loved companion,' he wrote to his wife two days later, 'by the will and grace of God, the Bastard and all those with him were discomforted, may Our Lord be thanked, and between five and six thousand of his army were killed and such an abundance of prisoners that we do not yet know all their names, but among others taken were Don Sancho brother of the said Bastard, the Count of Denia, Sir Bertram Duguesclin, the Marshal d'Audrehem . . ., and as many as two thousand men of quality . . . On Monday, that is to say the day on which this is written, we . . . moved on towards Burgos.'

The discovery of Audrehem among the prisoners roused the prince to anger. The elderly French marshal had been released from captivity after Poitiers on oath not to take arms against the King of England or the Prince of Wales (except in the defence of his own sovereign) until the whole of his ransom had been paid. Since there was a sum still owing, and since Charles V had been at great pains to disown any direct involvement in the Spanish conflict, Audrehem was, the prince told him to his face, forsworn and a traitor – an accusation in which was inherent the loss of all chivalrous privileges and condemnation to a shameful death.

Audrehem replied boldly: 'Sire, you are a King's son – therefore I cannot answer you as I might – but I am neither a traitor nor an oathbreaker.' The prince asked him if he would accept trial by a jury of twelve knights, four English, four Gascon and four Breton. When Audrehem assented, the court was convened and the prince repeated his formal accusation: 'Your ransom has not been paid, the King of France was not present at yesterday's battle, nor any person of his line, and yet in violation of your promises you armed yourself with all your weapons against me ... For that reason you are perjured.' There seemed to be no answer to the charge; the facts were common knowledge.

'Sire,' Audrehem replied, 'I beg that you will not take in bad part what I am about to say to justify myself, for this matter touches my honour and my word.' The prince assured him that he could speak without fear, since this was a question of chivalry. Audrehem then proceeded to admit that everything the prince had said was perfectly true – 'except,' he continued, 'that I did not take up arms against you, but against Don Pedro, on whose behalf you were employed to make war, having accepted his pay and wages ..., and in whose name the battle was fought.' Whereupon the members of the court of honour unanimously decided that Audrehem was not guilty, and, as the standard-bearer of the Knights of the Red Sash recorded: 'It greatly pleased the Prince and all the knights that the Marshal had found good grounds to excuse himself, for he was a worthy knight.'

The prince followed Don Pedro to Burgos, lodging outside the city at the convent of Las Huelgas where Henry of Trastamara had been proclaimed king a year before, while his brother John of Gaunt set up his headquarters in the Dominican monastery of San Pablo. The prince sent his father the charger that

THE SPANISH ADVENTURE

Henry had ridden during the battle before exchanging it for the lighter, swifter horse on which he had made his escape. By Windsor Herald he sent a full report: 'Whereby the Prince was greatly renowned and his cavalry and high enterprise much praised in all places that heard thereof, and specially in the Empire of Almaine and in the realm of England; for the Almains, Flemings and Englishmen said that the Prince of Wales was chief flower of all chivalry, and how that such a Prince was well worthy to govern all the world.' In London 'the burgesses made great solemnity and triumph for that victory, as they anciently were wont to do for Kings when they had overcome their enemies. And in France there were made lamentable sorrows.'

It was beginning to appear, though, that the victory might have been gained at too great a cost – not in men but in money. The prince had undertaken to pay the invasion force on Pedro's promise to repay him when he regained the throne of Castile. But Pedro would be in no position to meet his obligations until he had gained a firm hold on the country again; he also disputed the amount involved – which had reached the staggering sum of $2\frac{3}{4}$ million gold florins, five times as much as had been anticipated. In an atmosphere of increasing hostility between the former allies, the unemployed and unpaid troops began to help themselves. 'There were many who ate not bread although they were hungry, and yet they dared not, of a truth, attack towns nor castles, for the Prince had forbidden it,' recorded Chandos's herald. But eventually, 'though they should be hanged for it they had to do it perforce, for great famine compelled them'.

It was agreed that the prince should move his army southwest into the more fertile province of Valladolid and that Pedro should reaffirm his obligations in a solemn ceremony at the cathedral of Santa Maria in Burgos on 2 May. Significantly, the prince concentrated his troops around Las Huelgas and sent a large detachment to occupy the gate and adjoining walls where he entered the city – accompanied by five hundred men-at-arms. At the high altar Pedro swore to pay half his debt within four months and the remainder by next Easter Sunday. He then went off on a tour of his kingdom, seeking the money.

The prince waited, but Pedro did not return. The prince sent Sir Nigel Loring to Seville to inquire. Pedro was only too ready to explain: 'Certainly it displeaseth us that we cannot keep the promise that we have made with our cousin the Prince ..., but our people excuseth themselves and saith how they can make no sum of money as long as the Companions be in the country, for they have three or four times robbed our treasurers, who were coming to our cousin the Prince with our money.' In short, Pedro made it clear that he did not intend to pay the money unless the prince withdrew his troops from Castile. What was equally clear to the prince was that he had little chance of getting the money if he did withdraw them. When he sent Lord Poynings to Viscaya to take over the province that Pedro had given him, the Viscayans told Poynings that by ancient Basque custom they chose their own rulers – and did not intend to accept the prince. When Chandos claimed the fortress and estate of Soria – another gift from Pedro – he was told that he might certainly have it, but only after payment of a registration fee of 10,000 doublarms.

The summer sun of central Spain beat down on the restless, penniless army, its numbers now being drastically reduced by dysentery and other diseases. From Bordeaux the Princess of Wales sent warnings that Henry of Trastamara, with support from the Duke of Anjou, was preparing to take his revenge on the vulnerable eastern districts of Aquitaine. 'The Prince perceived clearly that King Don Pedro was not as loyal as he thought,' and decided to return to Bordeaux. By the end of August 1367 he was back at the archbishop's palace. 'The Princess came to meet him, bringing with her Edward her first born son ... Very sweetly they embraced when they met together. The gentle-hearted Prince kissed his wife and his son. They went to their lodging on foot, holding each other by the hand.'

He was thirty-seven years old, and suddenly broken in health and crippled with debts.

# Chapter Eight

# Trouble in Aquitaine

The princess's warnings were well founded. Shortly before the prince's return to Bordeaux, Henry of Trastamara and Louis of Anjou had signed a treaty at Aigues-Mortes under which Anjou promised to help Henry regain the throne of Castile, and Henry in return undertook to invade Aquitaine before the end of the following March. Long before he left Spain, the prince had determined to block Henry's re-entry into the peninsula by way of Aragon. He moved troops towards the Aragonese frontier, let the word spread that he was about to attack, then sent Hugh Calveley to negotiate. Calveley, who held the title of Count of Carrion from Peter, arrived at Saragossa towards the end of April 1367, and within a month obtained the king's assurance that he was ready to make defensive pacts with his neighbours Pedro and Carlos and deny passage through his kingdom to Henry and his French-financed mercenaries. By the time the definitive discussions began, however, it had become clear that Pedro had little intention of paying his debts. So while Peter and Pedro were signing their truce in mid-August, new emissaries from the prince were offering Peter a very different proposition: if Pedro had not surrendered the province of Viscaya to the prince and paid the money he owed him within a reasonable time, the prince would himself invade and seize the throne of Castile and would hand over the disputed territories bordering their kingdoms to the rulers of Aragon, Navarre and Portugal if they supported his action. What remained of Castile would become a new kingdom for the prince's son, Edward of Angoulême, who would marry Peter's daughter Leonor. One of Peter's tasks would be to interest Fernando the Handsome of Portugal (who had just succeeded his father, Pedro the Severe) in the project. Peter accepted the prince's invitation to send representatives to further discussions in October. So when the prince left Spain he could well feel that he had covered most possibilities. By denying Henry passage through Aragon he gave Pedro time enough to fulfil his promises. If Pedro failed to do this the prince would, by seizing Castile, obtain his rights and continue to deny use of the Castilian fleet to the French.

He was consequently outraged to learn at the beginning of October 1367 that Henry had reappeared at Calahorra and had crossed the river into Castile. The prince's immediate suspicion, that Peter of Aragon had betrayed their agreement, turned out to be incorrect. (When asked by Charles V to declare war on Pedro in favour of Henry, Peter had refused, querulously replying, 'for the one I wish great evil, and the other little good'.) Instead of marching along the coastal route through Roussillon, Henry had hired guides to take him over the distant mountains of the county of Foix, skirting Andorra, across to the Val d'Aran and then down the Navarre–Aragon border to the valley of the Ebro. Because of the difficulty of the mountain paths he followed he was able to bring no more than two or three thousand French mercenaries with him. To these he added some Castilians who had always opposed Pedro or had grown disillusioned.

Although the majority of the subjects that he once more claimed to call his own showed little eagerness to receive him, Henry entered Burgos without opposition, except from the ghetto (he was known to be fanatically anti-Jewish) and the garrison – which he punished ruthlessly. He was faced with a long campaign this time, conquering the country city by city, fortress by fortress, province by province, moving down towards Seville, where Pedro was strongest, but equally lacking in positive support from a country weary of civil war.

The prince's representatives agreed with those of Aragon and Navarre to send ultimatums to both Henry and Pedro, demanding satisfaction for all outstanding debts. The purpose was probably simply to obtain an excuse for intervening and dividing Castile between the three countries. The prince accepted the plan in principle but stipulated that his father must have the last word on a matter of such importance. Peter of Aragon sent

A gold *guiennois* minted by order of the Prince of Wales and Aquitaine and bearing his effigy.

a mission to Edward III early in 1368 for this purpose. Carlos of Navarre, taking advantage of the continuing indecisive struggle in Castile, sent troops in April that year to occupy the territory that Pedro had promised him at Libourne in 1366.

The Prince of Wales meanwhile summoned the Estates of Aquitaine to confer with him at Angoulême. There the chancellor, John Harewell, Bishop of Bath and Wells, explained the prince's need to levy a *fouage* (hearth tax) 'for the intent to raise such money as he ought by reason of his journey into Spain'. He proposed that it should run for five years and each household should pay ten sous. The Commons (many of them unaffected, since the larger cities had special privileges) agreed to the tax, subject to the prince's striking a new coinage and guaranteeing its value for five years, so that they should be certain what they were committing themselves to. (In France the business communities had suffered great losses through the royal juggling of the coinage: in the 1350s the *livre tournois* changed in value seventy-one times during the decade.)

The nobility of Aquitaine, however, were much less cooperative. Some insisted that the prince should first accept the principle that no taxation could be levied on their vassals without their consent as overlords; others made no comment but

185

resolved not to pay. Opposition came principally from those seigneurs whose estates lay nearest to France, and from those whom the prince had previously humiliated in war, such as the Count of Armagnac, or who had personal quarrels with him, such as Armagnac's nephew the Lord of Albret. There is no doubt that they were encouraged to defy him because they believed he was too ill to enforce his will. During the Spanish expedition he had contracted some disease which his doctors could neither name nor cure. Chandos Herald noted that it was at Angoulême that this sickness first became plainly apparent; and 'then began falsehood and treason to govern those who should have loved him, for those whom he held as his friends then became his enemies'.

In May 1368, the Lord of Albret married Marguerite of Bourbon, sister of the Queen of France. His uncle the Count of Armagnac attended the wedding, having gone to Paris to visit his son-in-law, King Charles's brother, the Duke of Berry. In this close family circle the final plans against the English were laid. It was agreed that Albret and Armagnac should appeal to Charles for a decision on their dispute with the Prince of Wales and that Charles should accept the appeal. Thus Charles would reassert his claim to be the prince's overlord. And the prince would have to accept this position or embark on a war that he had neither the health nor the money to fight. At the end of June 1368, Charles signed an agreement with Armagnac confirming their relationship as sovereign lord and vassal which neither would renounce without the other's consent. But for the moment this had to be kept secret. Charles had first to complete the encirclement of Aquitaine. In July he offered Henry of Trastamara more mercenaries in return for cooperation against the English. At the same time Duguesclin, who had been ransomed by Charles in January, tried to intimidate Peter of Aragon by marching his brigands on Roussillon. But Peter remained loyal to his engagements with Pedro, who was still holding out in southern Castile, and to the prince.

Although the various parties still preserved the diplomatic proprieties, they were all well aware of what the others were up to. In September 1368 Edward III sent ambassadors to Paris to protest at the delay in payment of the dead King Jean's ransom, the failure to replace hostages who had died or escaped, and the continued dispute over territories that should have been surrendered under the Treaty of Brétigny. But their principal mission was to demand that Charles should refuse to accept the appeals of the Gascon lords that he should settle their dispute (the Count of Périgord had now joined them) and cooperate with the English king in preserving the terms of the treaty. They could get no satisfactory answer. Later that month Armagnac repaid the balance of the money that the Prince of Wales had lent him to pay his ransom to the Count of Foix. At about the same time Rodez, capital city of Rouergue, renounced its allegiance to the prince. The word spread through Aquitaine that the King of France had set 19 October as the day for invasion on all fronts.

October came and went. Charles made no move. In December Duguesclin, denied passage through Aragon by King Peter, did as Henry of Trastamara had done – climbed over the Pyrenees and through the Val d'Aran to Navarre, where he created much havoc and frightened the queen into promising him estates in Normandy and giving him jewels which he pawned for 26,000 florins in Saragossa. At the end of December Charles consulted his council once more and made up his mind to send the Prince of Wales the decisive letter, which had in fact been drawn up more than a month before.

It was delivered to the palace in Bordeaux on 15 January 1369, by a French knight and a judge from the Parlement of Paris who had instructions to read it aloud to the prince. It contained the anticipated complaints of injustices to Albret, Armagnac, Périgord and other Gascon magnates who had joined them, but ended with a quite unexpected summons for the prince to appear in person before Charles and the Parlement of Paris to answer the charges.

At this public insult 'the Prince, who was ill, was mighty wroth. Then he raised himself from his bed and said, "Fair sirs, by my faith, methinks by what I see that the French hold me as dead; but, if God will comfort me and if I can rise from this bed, I will yet do them much hurt, for God knows well that they unjustly make complaint of me."' Addressing Charles's messengers directly, he added: 'Sirs, we will gladly go to Paris to our uncle, sith he has sent thus for us; but I assure you that it shall be with bassinet on our head and 60,000 men in our company.' Fighting broke out in the exposed province of Rouergue, bordered by France on three sides and inhabited by many vassals of the Count of Armagnac. The Count of Charolais, Armagnac's eldest son, advanced on Millau.

In central Spain Duguesclin linked up with Henry of Trastamara at Orgaz, twenty miles south of Toledo. Some eighty miles away Pedro had arrived at the fortress of the Order of Santiago at Montiel. He had come from his headquarters in Seville to relieve Toledo, whose citizens had remained loyal to him through a twelve month siege but were now reduced to eating horses, rats and, it was said, human flesh. He brought with him an army of 3,000 horsemen drawn largely from the southern provinces, together with 1,500 light cavalrymen lent him by Mohammed V, the Moorish King of Granada. He billeted them in the surrounding district while waiting to be joined by reinforcements from Murcia.

It was these that he assumed to be arriving when his lookouts reported distant moving lights at nightfall on 13 March 1369. But at dawn he was abruptly woken with the news that the whole of Henry's army – which he believed to be investing Toledo – was almost upon him, with Duguesclin leading the van. Pedro sent urgent summonses to his scattered troops and went out to meet the attack, accompanied only by the men-at-arms and crossbowmen of his household and the Moorish cavalry. Duguesclin, badly guided, lost his way in a ravine, so that it was the main body of Henry's army, under the usurper himself, that fell upon Pedro. They were seasoned troops and in far greater numbers than Pedro's. Pedro's scattered companies either met defeat piecemeal or ran away. Pedro 'fought valiantly with a great axe and gave therewith many a great stroke', but within an hour he was back inside the fortress of Montiel, 'so straitly watched day and night that a bird could not come out of the castle without spying'. But a messenger could be got out by arrangement, and Pedro sent word to Duguesclin that he would grant him six towns and 200,000 gold doubloons if the Breton leader helped him to escape. Some days later he received the reply: Duguesclin and his senior French captains solemnly swore to get Pedro safely through the lines.

In the night of Friday 23 March, Pedro left the fortress with a handful of companions. The besiegers' outposts let him pass unchallenged. Duguesclin was waiting for him. Pedro whispered, 'Come, Sir Bertrand – to horse! There is no time to lose!' There was no reply. Pedro tried to mount but found a man-at-arms obstructing him. He was surrounded by silent French mercenaries who hustled him away – perhaps to Duguesclin's tent, perhaps to a village house used as head-quarters by one of Duguesclin's lieutenants. He realized that Duguesclin had betrayed him to Henry in return for a greater reward.

At last Henry arrived, fully armed and armoured. It was fif-teen years since the half-brothers had met, when Henry was twenty and Pedro nineteen. 'Where is that whoreson and Jew that calleth himself King of Castile?' cried Henry. 'Nay, thou art a whoreson and I am son to King Alfonso!' Pedro shouted back. Henry drew his dagger and stabbed Pedro in the face. Pedro grappled 'and wrestled so with him that he overthrew him on a bench, and set his hand on his knife and had slain him without remedy, and the Viscount of Rocaberti had not been there. He took King Don Peter by the leg and turned him up-se-down, so that King Henry was then above, who drew out a long knife and strake King Don Peter into the body. Therewith his men came in to help him.' When the murder was completed, Henry cut off his brother's head and sent it to Seville. The reward that he gave to Duguesclin was well deserved. Rumour said it was Duguesclin himself, or his cousin Olivier de Mauny – not Rocaberti – who twisted Pedro over to receive the thrust of Henry's knife.

In Bordeaux a representative of Peter of Aragon came to in-quire whether the prince was of a mind to intervene in Spain as they had previously agreed. He was – but he needed time, for the outbreak of disobedience in Gascony was spreading day by day. In Quercy the Bishop of Toulouse was vigorously preaching rebellion against the English. Cahors and Villeneuve declared for Charles despite the formidable oaths their citizens had taken to be loyal to the prince: 'on the Holy Gospels of God, on the Sign of the Cross, on our Baptism, on our Faith,

189

Duguesclin,
returned from
Spain and his part
in the murder of
Pedro the Cruel, is
appointed
Constable of
France by Charles
V.

on our Share of Paradise, on the Damnation of our Souls, for ourselves, our heirs and successors.'

The prince summoned help from Chandos (who had gone to his estates at Saint-Sauveur-le-Vicomte, reputedly after disagreeing with the prince over the wisdom of imposing the *fouage*) and such other famous captains as Robert Knollys, Eustace d'Auberchicourt, James Audley and the Captal de Buch. The prince's brother, Edmund Earl of Cambridge, arrived from England with John Hastings Earl of Pembroke, husband of their sister Margaret, bringing reinforcements. These counter-raided into the territories of the rebellious lords – Armagnac, Périgord, Albret – and into Anjou and Berry. But the tables were turned now. Territories and towns are more easily taken than held. The grasp had exceeded the grip. It was no longer a matter of military skill but of numbers and, in this war which did so much to rouse and nurture it, of nationality. Willy-nilly – and there were many, especially in the towns, who believed themselves to have been better treated by the English than the French – the 'new Gascons' who had changed masters under the Treaty of Brétigny were wooed or intimidated into resuming allegiance to France.

On 14 May 1369, seated on his four-poster ceremonial Bed of Justice, beneath a blue velvet tester sprinkled with golden fleurs de lys, Charles proclaimed to his Parlement that he had resumed direct suzerainty over the duchy of Aquitaine. The following day he declared all property held in Guienne by Englishmen to be forfeit to the French crown. On 3 June Edward met *his* Parliament, who declared him released from all obligations under the Treaties of Brétigny and Calais, and at liberty to resume the title of King of France. As King of France Edward announced that all lands not belonging to the crown or the church would become the property of any who conquered them – an open invitation for the Free Companies to help themselves. Parliament voted him additional taxes on wool and hides for three years. Edward prepared for outright war again, and on 18 June ensured the safety of his northern frontier by signing a fifteen-year truce with the King of Scotland.

At Harfleur, Charles amassed great stores of wheat, wine, bacon and salt fish, and fodder and nosebags for horses. Men were encamped in readiness along the Seine. The fleet to carry this army across the Channel was being prepared at the Clos des Galées, the royal shipyard at Rouen. It is not certain whether Charles had planned a full-scale invasion of England or a series of heavy raids to cover his attacks on English territory on the Continent. In any event, Edward forestalled him. At the beginning of July he sent a raiding force to Harfleur; at the end of the month the twenty-nine-year-old John of Gaunt Duke of Lancaster took some 600 men-at-arms and 1,500 archers – his first independent command – to Calais and from there went on *chevauchée* through Picardy. Charles's brother Philippe, the young hero of Poitiers whom King Jean had made Duke of Burgundy, was sent to oppose Lancaster with the expeditionary army from the Seine.

On 25 August the two armies took up battle positions outside

191

Tournehem. Philippe was under orders to follow his brother's policy of never entering into a pitched battle against the English. Lancaster was fulfilling his mission by immobilizing Philippe. It was stalemate. Philippe's men, disgruntled by shortages of pay, began to desert. Philippe himself, keenly embarrassed – he had been nicknamed Le Hardi, the Bold – on 12 September ordered his diminishing army to turn about and marched them back into Normandy. Lancaster followed, burning his way to Saint-Pol, back to Saint-Riquier, across the Somme at Blanche-Taque, then down the coast, accompanied by the fleet that had brought him to Calais. The ships, tracing his progress by the pillars of fire and smoke, put in at convenient intervals to take on board his accumulations of booty. Lancaster pushed right down to the Seine, burned Sainte-Adresse, the port that later developed into Le Havre, and threatened Harfleur, which he could not take for lack of siege engines. He returned on a parallel route of destruction to Calais and was back in England by November.

While the prince's brother Lancaster was raiding down into Normandy, his brother-in-law Pembroke thrust upward to the borders of Poitou and captured La Roche-sur-Yon; but at the other end of Aquitaine, succumbing to bribes from the Duke of Anjou, the burgesses of the key town of Montauban submitted to the King of France. Late in December 1369, Chandos, the Seneschal of Poitou, set out with three hundred men-at-arms to recapture Saint-Savin-sur-Gartempe. Failing to surprise the town with a night attack, Chandos sent most of his force back the twenty-five miles to Poitiers and himself settled down to pass the rest of the night in a large house at Chauvigny. Just before dawn he was told that a strong party of French men-at-arms had been seen riding out of Saint-Savin. Chandos ordered his forty men to saddle up. He overtook the Frenchmen at Lussac.

Though greatly outnumbered, Chandos dismounted his men and led them into the attack. 'The same morning there had fallen a great dew, so that the ground was somewhat moist, and so in his going forward he slid and fell down at the joining with his enemies; and as he was arising there lit a stroke on him ... which entered into the flesh under his eye between the nose and the forehead. Sir John Chandos saw not the stroke coming

'This noble Knight, Sir John Chandos: in a hundred year past there was not a more courteous nor more fuller of noble virtues.'

on that side, for he was blind on the one eye. He lost the sight thereof a five year before, as he hunted an hart in the launds of Bordeaux, and also he had on no visor. The stroke was rude and entered into his brain, the which stroke grieved him so sore that he overthrew to the earth and turned for pain two times up-se-down, as he that was wounded for death; for after the stroke he never spake word.' Captured by the French but almost immediately rescued by two hundred loyal Poitevins,

193

Chandos was stripped of his armour and carried on shields to Morthemer, the next fortress down the river. 'And this noble Knight, Sir John Chandos, lived not after his hurt past a day and a night, but so died. God have mercy on his soul: for in a hundred year past there was not a more courteous nor more fuller of noble virtues.'

The prince had lost the sturdiest of his commanders and companions. It was a year of melancholy and mortality. Sir James Audley had died of a sickness at La Roche-sur-Yon a month or two earlier. In September his sister-in-law Blanche, who had brought John of Gaunt the title of Lancaster, succumbed to the plague. Less than a month before, his mother, the gentle, gracious Philippa, had died. 'Thus every kind of mischance arose,' wrote Chandos Herald; 'one after another they fell upon the noble Prince, who lay ill in bed. [Modern medical opinion has diagnosed amoebic dysentery contracted in Spain, complicated by chronic nephritis.] But despite all this he gave thanks to God and said: "All things will have their season; if I could rise from here I would take good vengeance."'

As was to be expected, Carlos of Navarre was already fishing in these troubled waters, conducting simultaneous secret negotiations with Edward and Charles. By the spring of 1370 it was agreed that an army that Edward was assembling should go to Normandy and join forces that Carlos would raise there. But when the expedition, some four or five thousand strong, set sail in July, the ships were driven off course and the leader, Sir Robert Knollys, had to be satisfied with the friendly port nearest to where the wind carried him – Calais. Towards the end of July he set off on a *chevauchée* through Artois, Picardy, Vermandois and Champagne. In Paris Charles called a conference to consider how to strike a decisive blow against the English. For his Gascon allies there was no attraction in fighting over their own and each other's estates. They had joined him on the promise of increased privileges. If they did not soon receive them, in conditions in which they could enjoy them, they were quite likely to defect back to the other side.

It was common knowledge that the prince was lying sick at Angoulême. Charles's council decided on a bold move to capture him. The Duke of Anjou was to strike north from Toulouse through the Agenais and Périgord, and Berry would ad-

vance west through the Limousin. They set off in July and
scored a succession of victories. By late August the Duke of
Anjou, reinforced by Duguesclin and the Breton mercenaries
he had brought back from Spain, was at Périgueux, fifty-five
miles south-east of Angoulême, and Berry at Limoges, scarcely
farther to the east. The prince had withdrawn to Cognac, which
he appointed as the rallying place for all his available forces.
It was there that he learned that the citizens of Limoges had
surrendered to the Duke of Berry's troops. They had been persuaded to this act of treason by their bishop who had recently
returned from Angoulême and told them that he 'had seen the
Prince put into his shroud, and could affirm that he was
dead'.

The news roused and enraged the wounded lion. The bishop,
Jean de Cros, was not only one of the prince's most trusted coun-
sellors but also a close friend: 'his gossip', the god-parent of the
prince's eldest son. It was because of this that the prince had
appointed him governor of Limoges. It offended the prince's
deepest principles that a man of God should break so many
solemn oaths and bonds of friendship and pervert a great city
into a similar breach of faith. 'Then he sware by his father's
soul ... that he would get it again and 'that he would make
the traitors dearly abye their falseness.'

The prince's army included many and varied contingents.
There were Poitevins such as Guichard d'Angle, who had
served with King Jean at Poitiers but with the prince at Nájera
and was shortly to be made Knight of the Garter and later Earl
of Huntingdon. There were Gascons under Guillaume Sans
Lord of Pommiers, Raymond of Montaut Lord of Mussidan,
and Jean de Grailly Captal de Buch. There were such famous
English names as Neville and Percy and Beauchamp, Stephen
Cossington who had been a marshal at Nájera, and Simon
Burley the kinsman of the prince's tutor and destined to be
appointed to the same post with the prince's son Richard. There
were Hainaulters under Eustace d'Auberchicourt who commanded a freelance company that he took to Spain with
Duguesclin but later brought back to fight on the other side,
for the prince, at Nájera. Auberchicourt had in 1360 married
the dowager Countess of Kent, Isabella of Juliers, niece of
Queen Philippa and sister-in-law of the prince's wife Joan.

Closer relations serving under the prince were his brother-in-law the Earl of Pembroke, his brother Edmund Earl of Cambridge and – newly arrived from England – his brother the Duke of Lancaster. The duke, who received a salary of 26s 8d a day, brought with him three bannerets at 8s a day, eighty knights at 4s, 216 men-at-arms at 2s and 500 archers at 12d. The inflationary pressures of war and the Black Death had doubled the rates of pay in fifteen years.

'So all these men of war went forth in good ordinance and took the fields, and all the country trembled before them. The Prince was so diseased that he could not ride, but so was carried in a horse litter.' Yet even when sick he still inspired fear in his enemies. The Bishop of Limoges, learning of the approach of the prince's army, sent messengers to the Duke of Berry, begging him to return. (Berry had spent no more than a day or two in the city before withdrawing northward to his duchy, leaving some of his men as garrison.) The duke turned a deaf and cowardly ear.

The prince arrived in front of Limoges on 14 September 1370. The town opened its gates to him. The more strongly fortified *cité* or bourg, containing the bishop's palace, refused the prince's summons to surrender. 'He had always in his company a great number of miners, and so he set them a-work to undermine.' The men, possibly drawn from the tin mines of his duchy of Cornwall, dug beneath the walls, shoring up their tunnel with wooden props. On 18 September 1370 they reported that the work was complete. The prince ordered that '"Tomorrow betimes ye shew forth and execute your work." Then the miners set fire unto their mine, and so the next morning, as the Prince had ordained, there fell down a great pane of the wall and filled the dikes, whereof the Englishmen were glad and were ready armed in the field to enter the town. The footmen might well enter at their ease. And so they did and ran to the gate and beat down the fortifying and the barriers, for there was no defence against them; it was done so suddenly that those of the town were not aware thereof.'

It was – exactly to the day – the fourteenth anniversary of the prince's victory at Poitiers. But his treatment of the Bishop of Limoges was far different from the humble courtesy that he had shown to the defeated King of France. 'A certain company of

Englishmen entered into the Bishop's palace and there they
found the Bishop; and so they brought him to the Prince's presence, who beheld him right fiercely and felly, and the best word
he could have of him was, how he would have his head stricken
off, and so he was had out of his sight.' The attackers proceeded
with the sack of the city. 'It was great pity to see the men,
women and children that kneeled down on their knees before
the Prince for mercy; but he was so inflamed with ire that he
took no heed to them, so that none was heard but all put to
death...: for more than three thousand men, women and
children were slain and beheaded that day.'

Jean de Cros,
Bishop of Limoges,
was appointed
Cardinal after his
betrayal of the
Prince of Wales.
He is here
presenting a
message from the
Pope to Charles V.

197

The passage from Froissart is famous and familiar. The French, who never forgot or forgave the prince's victories, have suggested that it was the massacre at Limoges that earned him the nickname Black. The accusation of inhuman brutality has been repeated often enough to be worth correcting. There is no need to defend the prince with a plea of exaggeration – though it is now accepted that Froissart multiplied the number of dead tenfold. ('The City was taken and burned and more than 300 persons put to death because of the rebellion they had made against Sir Edward of Aquitaine,' recorded the contemporary local chronicler of the abbey of Saint-Martial.) Nor does the prince need sheltering behind the argument that there are many examples of similar and worse massacres by others – the 'Butcher' Clisson, for instance, who changed sides twice and, after accepting the surrender of the English garrison of Benon, stood at the castle door and hacked off the head of each man as he emerged. The position at Limoges was quite clear: the city had been given the opportunity to surrender and had refused. Under the established conventions of the time, if the defenders rejected such an offer, and their attackers undertook the risks of assaulting an enemy protected by high walls and fixed artillery (in itself an outrage to the old chivalric idea of equal combat between man and man with sword or lance), then in the event of defeat the defenders became the sole property of the victors – as they had been at Calais in 1347, and in countless other instances. It was always open to the defenders to offer to surrender on terms which would at least guarantee their lives.

It sometimes happened that the opposing forces came to an agreement – that the besieged would submit to the besiegers with honour and without penalty if they had not been relieved within a stated time. The purpose of this was to prevent heavy losses to the attackers and to avoid loss of honour by the defenders who had sworn to preserve the fortress for the sovereign who employed them. If he did not come to their rescue within a reasonable time they were quit of their word. (Rescue clauses of this kind were inserted in the contracts that King Edward signed when he sent the prince, Lancaster and others on service abroad.) But here we are touching on the special and most grave source of the prince's anger: the Limou-

sins were not protecting the sanctity of their oath to a distant
overlord – they were by the very act of resistance to the prince
breaking the solemn word by which they had sworn to be faith-
ful to him. The sanctity of the oath was central to chivalry.
It was for this reason that he had insisted that the elderly and
respected Marshal Audrehem should appear before a court of
honour and clear himself of the charge of breaking his sworn
word by fighting at Nájera. Such an action was an affront to
his deepest principles.

The garrison commander Jean de Villemur, his lieutenant
Hugues de la Roche, and a squire Roger Beaufort, who was
nephew of the new Pope Gregory XI, decided to ' "sell our lives
dearly, as good knights ought to do" ... They assembled their
men together in a place against an old wall and there displayed
their banners. So they were to the number of eighty persons.
Thither came the Duke of Lancaster, the Earl of Cambridge
and their companies and so lighted afoot, so that the
Frenchmen could not long endure against the Englishmen, for
anon they were slain and taken. Howbeit, the Duke of Lancaster fought long hand to hand against Sir Jean de Villemur,
who was a strong knight and a hardy, and the Earl of Cambridge fought against Sir Hugues de la Roche and the Earl of
Pembroke against Roger Beaufort.

'These three Frenchmen did many feats of arms ... The
Prince in his chariot came by them and beheld them gladly.'
His admiration for their bravery was so great that he 'appeased
himself in the beholding of them'. Their display of chivalry
saved the remaining inhabitants of the city. The prince ordered
his men to halt the retribution they were visiting upon the forsworn Limousins. He let his brother Lancaster take charge of
the faithless bishop (whom Lancaster later allowed to go to
Avignon to join his cousin, Pope Gregory). Exhausted with ill-
ness and spent anger he had himself carried back to Cognac,
'where my Lady the Princess was. Then the Prince gave leave
for all his men of war to depart and did no more that season;
for he felt himself not well at ease, for always his sickness increased, whereof his brethren and people were sore dismayed.'

It was evident – even to him, now – that he could no longer
support the burden of ruling Aquitaine. When Lancaster came

from England in the summer he had brought permission from their father to help the prince in any way whatever. On 11 October 1370, at Cognac, the prince appointed his brother as his lieutenant in Aquitaine. Lancaster, who did not intend to get engulfed in the Gascon morass of shifting loyalties and shattered finance, stipulated that he would deputize only until the following June – and was at liberty to quit (handing over his authority to the constable, the Captal de Buch, and the seneschal, Sir Thomas Felton) at any time before that if his troops' pay fell more than a month in arrears.

At Bordeaux the prince presented his brother to a Parliament of those Gascon lords who still remained loyal. The winter brought storms and foul weather, but his doctors insisted that if his life was to be preserved at all he must return to England. He sailed in January 1371, his last days in Aquitaine made even more bitter by the death of his elder child, Edward of Angoulême. The voyage to Plymouth with his beautiful wife and pretty four-year-old son Richard was made with unexpected ease and speed, but on landing he had to take to his bed once more and it was not until April that he was able to continue to London. He reported to his father at Windsor and then went to his estate at Berkhamsted.

*Opposite* All Souls College, Oxford. A portrait of John of Gaunt in a stained-glass window erected about forty years after his death.

Chapter Nine

# 'So Decreased and Destroyed...'

It was a sad homecoming. After Queen Philippa's death – or
possibly some years before it – the king had become infatuated
with one of her ladies-in-waiting, a woman named Alice Perrers. She was undistinguished in looks but quickwitted and
ambitious. Her success in enslaving Edward aroused alarm and
envy in his council and Parliament, sorrow and contempt
among the rest of his subjects: 'for as in his beginning all things
were joyful and liking to him and to all the people, and in his
middle-age he passed all men in high joy and worship and
blessedness, right so when he drew into age, drawn downward
through lechery and other sins, little by little all those joyful
and blessed things, good fortune and prosperity, decreased and
misshaped, and unfortunate things and unprofitable harms
with much evil, began to spring.'

Among other 'unfortunate things', there was a revival of invasion scares. In December 1369 King Charles had provided
Owen of Wales with a fleet and army to invade the Principality, but the ships were dispersed and driven back to port
by a severe storm. In November 1370 it was learned that a
new expedition was being assembled on the Seine. Meanwhile
the mayor, aldermen and commonalty of the City of London
had been warned that 'certain galleys with a multitude of
armed men therein, were lying off the Foreland of Thanet'.
They consequently ordered 'that every night in future ... watch
should be kept between the Tower of London and Billingsgate
by 40 men-at-arms and 60 archers' who were to be provided
by the various trades: 'On Tuesday the Drapers and the
Tailors. On Wednesday the Mercers and the Apothecaries. On

Thursday the Fishmongers and the Butchers. On Friday the Pelterers and the Vintners. On Saturday the Goldsmiths and the Saddlers. On Sunday the Ironmongers, the Armourers and the Cutlers. On Monday the Tawyers, the Spurriers, the Bowyers and the Girdlers.' There was good reason for the precautions: it was less than a year since Portsmouth had been pillaged and burned by French raiders.

The news from across the sea was no more encouraging. In Normandy Knollys had been defeated by Duguesclin, recently appointed Constable of France. In Aquitaine the Duke of Lancaster was busy with sieges and counter-attacks; but there was no concealing the truth that each time the Duke returned to Bordeaux some new town or estate defected to the French. Beyond England's agitated northern border, David died in February 1371 and was succeeded by Robert Fitzflaald, 7th High Steward of Scotland, grandson in the female line of Robert de Bruce, and founder of the Stuart dynasty. Charles V lent him 100,000 gold nobles to pay off David's ransom and so end the truce with England and promised him armour for 1,000 men.

Parliament, meeting in March 1371, was so impressed by the chancellor's description of the French preparations for full-scale war that it voted the king a levy of 22s 3d from every parish. This rate was increased to 116s in June after the discovery that there were only 8,600 parishes in the kingdom instead of 40,000 as had been assumed – a typical example of the lack of elementary statistical information which made the operation of central government so difficult in the Middle Ages. But although Parliament paid heed to the report presented by the lord chancellor, William of Wykeham, Bishop of Winchester, it was opposed to the man himself. A longstanding dissatisfaction with the greed, arrogance and immorality of the clergy was aggravated by the setbacks abroad and the manifest partiality of the papacy for the French cause. A strong faction in the Lords and Commons, led by the prince's brother-in-law, the Earl of Pembroke, demanded that no clerics be allowed to hold the great offices of state. The king, not yet so sunk in dotage as to accept instructions from Parliament, refused to take action – though he used the threat of it to extract from the Convocations of York and Canterbury a contribution of £50,000 to his war fund.

*Opposite* Edward
III – 'when he drew
into age, drawn
downward through
lechery and other
sins'.

The bad odour which surrounded the king did not spread to his eldest son. The crippled warrior retained the respect and affection of the nation as both man and prince. In January 1370 'the Mayor, Aldermen and an immense Commonalty voted that there should be levied on the men of the Wards a fifteenth and half a fifteenth for two presents to be made to Edward Prince of Wales and to the Princess his consort at their return to England from Gascony'. They bought him a magnificent set of gold and silver vessels to replace those that he had melted down to pay his soldiers' wages. They included 18 pots, 9 basins, 6 ewers, 36 hanaps (drinking vessels with handles), 20 chargers, 120 porringers and 60 saltcellars, and cost nearly £700. To the princess they gave 500 marks.

By the spring of 1372 the king had collected much of the money that had been voted him and was actively preparing to make another descent on the Continent. But Charles's forces were making headway, too. In June 1372 the Earl of Pembroke, recently appointed lieutenant in Gascony, sailed for Bordeaux with troops and sufficient money to pay 3,000 soldiers for a year. Off La Rochelle he was intercepted by a Castilian fleet sent by Henry of Trastamara to help the French. After a battle lasting two days all the English ships were sunk or taken. Pembroke was made prisoner and his surviving men, fettered and dragged on leashes like dogs, were sent to rot in the dreaded Spanish prisons. This disaster was an unplanned prelude to a general French attack on Poitou, which had hitherto remained loyal to Edward. On 7 August Duguesclin and the Duke of Berry entered Poitiers.

A fortnight later Edward was at Preston, between Wingham and Sarre, waiting for his troops to gather at Sandwich. With those who had been ordered to embark at Southampton he was estimated to have 4,000 men-at-arms and 10,000 archers, carried in 400 ships. His aim was to reinforce La Rochelle, or to recapture it if it had already fallen, and thus retain a major port above Bordeaux. He had summoned all the great lords of the kingdom. John of Gaunt had brought every trained man from his many estates; the Prince of Wales insisted on leaving his sick-bed to take part in the expedition. It was all in vain. They sailed on 30 August and were at once confronted with fierce, adverse winds. Though they persevered for several weeks, the scattered ships were eventually forced to give up and allow themselves to be blown back into English ports. By this time the inhabitants of La Rochelle had driven out the English garrison and invited Duguesclin to enter. The other towns of Poitou and Saintonge toppled in succession: Saintes, Angoulême, Saint-Jean-d'Angély. The prince, his health finally and hopelessly broken, on 5 October surrendered to his father his title of Prince of Aquitaine.

When Parliament met in November, the Lords and Commons were loud in their criticism of both the king and the Church, although Edward had now dismissed Wykeham and other prelates and replaced them with laymen. They complained that 'twenty years since, the Navy of the Kingdom was ... so noble and so plentiful that all countries deemed and called our Lord *The King of the Sea* ... And now it is so decreased and destroyed ... that there hardly remains enough to defend the country.' It was a time of disillusion, of carping, of the loss of old friends. In December the Captal de Buch was led captive to Paris. Charles V put him in prison where he was to die four years later. In the spring of 1373, the French moved into Brittany, driving the duke to take refuge in England.

Edward mounted a new expedition, this time under John of Gaunt. When he set out from Calais on 4 August 1373, Gaunt's army, with numerous Almain mercenaries, was said to total between 11,000 and 16,000. He ravaged the land of France, but could not force the French to fight, even though he marched into the heart of the country and out again – down to Troyes, into the Auvergne, on to Bordeaux. Bitter weather came to the aid of the French, who followed on flanks and rear, pouncing on stragglers but never accepting battle. 'Let them go,' said Charles. 'Though a storm and tempest rage together over a land, they disperse of themselves. So will it be with the English.' When the duke and his men limped into the Gascon capital in December, three hundred of his knights were on foot. They had lost their horses and, unable to march under the weight of their armour, they had thrown it into rivers and ravines to prevent the French getting it. Of the long baggage train filled with booty, two-thirds had been abandoned on the way. In April 1374 the duke returned to England. In June came a new humiliation: Henry of Trastamara, by agreement with Carlos

'Twenty years since the Navy of this Kingdom was so noble and ... so plentiful that all countries deemed and called our Lord *The King of the Sea*.' The coin struck to commemorate the Battle of Sluys shows the victorious Edward III standing in a ship.

of Navarre, came up through the pass of Roncesvalles and laid seige to Bayonne; but the Duke of Anjou failed to take the concerted action that he had promised, and after a few days Henry withdrew.

By the autumn of 1374 the great principality of Aquitaine had shrunk to little more than the pales of Bordeaux and Bayonne. In the following year the fighting shifted to Brittany and Normandy but was brought to a temporary halt by a year's truce signed at Bruges on 27 June 1375 between the Dukes of Lancaster, Anjou and Berry. In England a warm spring developed into a hot summer and the hot summer into a terrible drought that ruined crops and killed off livestock.

Parliament met at the end of April 1376 – for the first time since 1373. Its members were seething with resentment at corruption at home and defeat abroad, at shortages, taxes, and labour problems. When the chancellor opened the debate with an outline of the purposes for which the king would require more money, he was at once faced with a demand for a thorough investigation of the conduct of the king's council, and the prosecution of all ministers found guilty of misconduct and fraud. Behind the men accused of misusing their official positions stood the figure of the king's mistress, Alice Perrers, more hated than ever since he had given her the late queen's jewels – an avowal of her hold over him and an insult to the memory of the much loved Philippa.

Neither Edward, who was ill at Eltham, nor the Prince of Wales, now virtually bed-ridden for most of the time, was able to attend at Westminster. The Speaker of the Commons denounced the peculators who had misused public funds to such an extent that, though a vast amount of money had been collected in taxes over the years, 'it is evident that neither the King nor the realm had any profit thereby'. John of Gaunt, the senior

207

The capture of the
Captal de Buch at
the Siege of
Soubise.

active member of the royal family, was at first inclined to deal
high-handedly with 'these base and ignoble knights – do they
think they be Kings or Princes of this land?' but was dissuaded
by his advisers, who warned him of the 'helpes these knights
... have to undershore them, for they have the favour and the
love of the lords, and specially of the Lord Edward Prince, your
brother, who giveth them his counsel and aid effectually'.

One reason why the brothers found themselves on opposing
sides was because Lancaster had spent more time at home in
contact with his father and the corrupt ministers. The duke was
closely linked with the chamberlain, William Lord Latimer,
who was accused not only of setting up an import monopoly
in association with a London merchant, Richard Lyons, 'setting
prices at their own pleasure, whereupon they have made such
a great scarcity ... that the common sort of people can scantly
live', but also of having received bribes for the surrender of
castles in Brittany to the French. Such corruption was
abhorrent to the prince, though evidently widespread in court
and city circles, for Lyons, 'fearing his own skin', was foolish
enough to offer the prince a bribe – sending him a barrel con-

John of Gaunt
arrives at Calais for
his expedition of
1373.

taining £1,000 disguised 'as if it had been a barrel of sturgeon'.
The prince sent it back and Lyons found himself clapped in
gaol.

The contempt that the prince felt for his brother's associates
was matched by his disgust at his father's thraldom to Alice
Perrers. There was nothing in the code of chivalry to which
he subscribed that forbade adultery, but the true knight was
expected to act in a seemly fashion – and this the king had
shamefully failed to do. He had flaunted his infatuation with
this woman who was said to be a weaver's daughter. Only two
years before he had let her lead the procession from the Tower
along the Cheap to the jousting ground at West Smithfield,
attired as the 'Lady of the Sun . . ., accompanied of many lords
and ladies, every lady leading a lord by his horse-bridle', and
there to preside at the seven-day tournament. Now she was
openly accused of interfering with the course of justice, sitting
on the bench with the judges and beating down any opposition
by appeals to the king, so that the Commons expressly
demanded 'that no woman should do so henceforward, and
especially Alice Perrers, under penalty . . . of being banished

209

from the kingdom'. No King of England had ever before been
so boldly addressed by his Parliament. This in itself greatly dis-
tressed the prince, who was certainly no democrat. But most
painful of all was the public humiliation of this lecherous old
man who was still his father and had for so long been his hero,
the mirror of all that was strong and noble and valiant and
honourable.

For more than five years the prince had been 'visited with
a great and incommodious disease of his body ..., which made
him many times so feeble that his servants took him very often
for dead. Yet he bore all these things with such patience that
he never seemed to offer unto God one mutinous word.' But
at the back of his mind there was a great fear – for the future
of his wife and son. In 1372 his brother John of Gaunt had
married Pedro the Cruel's daughter Constance and, in her
right, assumed the title of King of Castile. There was no possibility of his ever winning Castile, but he was popularly believed
to have designs on another throne, much closer at hand. It was
said that when his father and his brother died, he intended to
snatch the crown from the prince's son Richard, by pressure
on Parliament or, if necessary, by poison.

The prince was approaching his forty-sixth birthday. Even
in a much less superstitious age this would have seemed a por-
tentous time. At six years old he had been created the first duke
in English history; at sixteen he had won fame by the leading
rôle he played in the miracle of Crécy; at twenty-six he had
astonished Europe by capturing the King of France at Poitiers;
at thirty-six he had sealed his supremacy as a military leader
with the victory at Nájera. Early in June 1376 his condition
visibly worsened. He was dying; not as a warrior of wounds
or in the heat of battle, nor as a king anointed and full of years,
but wasted by a base disease, his glory long past, his tale un-
completed, neither young nor old, in a land that had once
glowed and rung to his prowess and was now sour, sullen,
divided and dark.

On Saturday 7 June he had his clerks draw up his testament
'in our chamber within the Palace of our redoubtable lord and
father the King at Westminster ... First we bequeath our soul
to God our Creator, and to the Holy Blessed Trinity, and
to the Glorious Virgin Mary, and to all the Saints.' To the

cathedral at Canterbury, where he directed that his body should be buried, he gave his breviary and missal and a Hall of ostrich plumes on black tapestry. To the monastery he had founded at Ashridge and the chapel of his castle at Wallingford he left his great altar of silver and gold, encrusted with rubies, sapphires and pearls and inlaid with a cross made from the wood of the True Cross, together with other religious articles and all his clothing with the exception of the blue gown embroidered with gold roses and ostrich plumes which he gave to his son Richard, and with it the matching bed that had been given him by the king. Richard also received 'our great bed with the embroidered angels', and the prince's newest bed in red silk with baudkin stripes (silk weft and gold warp), a Hall of arras and another of worsted. A red worsted Hall embroidered with eagles and griffins was left to 'our consort the Princess', and a silk bed to one of the prince's illegitimate sons, Sir Roger de Clarendon.

He was humble before God but with no false modesty before men. He decreed that his tomb should be set ten feet from the altar in the chantry chapel that he had built in the cathedral at Canterbury after his marriage to his dear Jeanette. It was to be 'made of good masonry, in marble. And we desire that around the tomb shall be twelve latten escutcheons, each a foot wide, six with our arms entire, and the other six of ostrich plumes and on each ... shall be written *homout*', and on top 'an image in copper-gilt relief in memory of us'. Then, having detailed the manner in which 'our body shall be led through the town of Canterbury unto the Priory', he signed the will and ordered the door of his room to be opened and his household brought in.

'Sirs,' he said, 'pardon me, for, by my faith, you have loyally served me yet I cannot of myself give each of you his reward – but God, by his most Holy name, will give it you in Holy Heaven. I commend my son to you, who is young and small, and beg you to serve him as loyally as you have served me.' It was this thought that dominated his last moments – a premonition, perhaps, of the violent fate that awaited the young, small Richard at the hands of the Lancastrians. 'He called the King his father and the Duke of Lancaster his brother; he commended to them his wife and his son, whom he greatly loved,

*Overleaf* 'I humbly beseech Thy mercy to give me remission of those sins which I have wickedly committed against Thee; and of all mortal men whom willingly or ignorantly I have offended, with all my heart I desire forgiveness.'

and begged them that each should help them. Each swore it on the Book and freely promised to aid his child and maintain him in his right.'

He was sinking fast. The following day (8 June 1376), 'the feast of the Holy Trinity ..., about 3 of the clock ..., he began vehemently to faint and so to lose his strength that scarce any breath remained in him, which the Bishop of Bangor, who was present, perceiving, he came unto him and said, "Now, without doubt, death is at hand ..., therefore I counsel you, my lord, now to forgive all those that have offended you."' The prince managed to say 'I will', but could not make any other intelligible sound, notwithstanding the pleas of the bishop who told

him: 'It sufficeth not to say only "I will" ..., you ought to ask pardon.' The prince, despite his struggles, could not utter another word. The bishop realized that evil spirits were at work: 'taking the sprinkle, he cast holy water by the four corners of the chamber where he lay, and behold, suddenly the Prince with joined hands and eyes lifted up to Heaven said: "I give thee thanks, O God, for all Thy benefits, and with all the pain of my soul I humbly beseech Thy mercy to give me remission of those sins which I have wickedly committed against Thee; and of all mortal men whom willingly or ignorantly I have offended, with all my heart I desire forgiveness." When he had spoken these words, he gave up the ghost.'

215

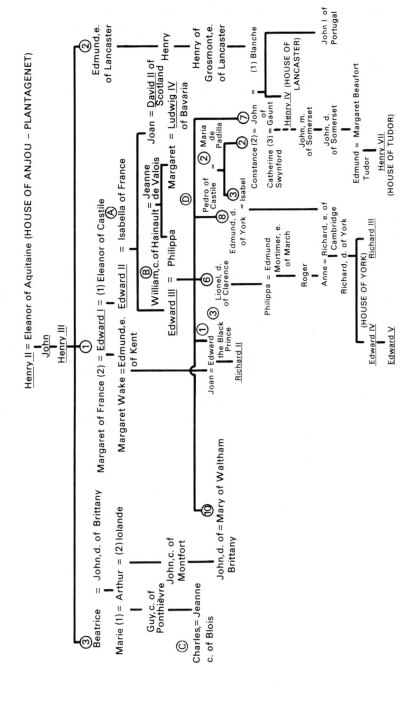

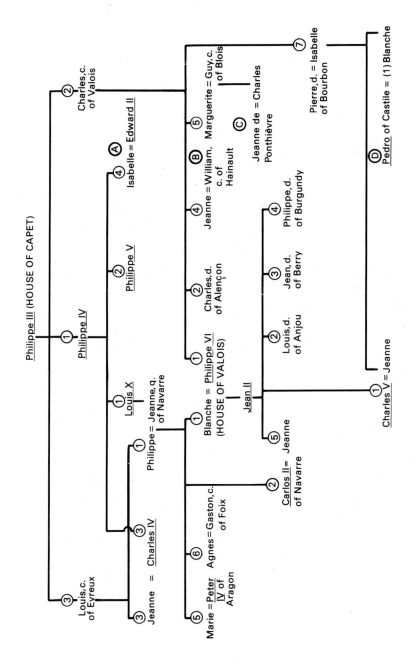

Philippe III (HOUSE OF CAPET)

① Philippe IV    ② Charles, c. of Valois    ③ Louis, c. of Evreux

① Louis X   ② Philippe V   ④ Isabelle = Edward II Ⓐ

③ Jeanne = Charles IV

Philippe = Jeanne, q. of Navarre ①

Agnes = Gaston, c. of Foix ⑥   Marie = Peter IV of Aragon ⑤

Blanche = Philippe VI (HOUSE OF VALOIS) ①   Charles, d. of Alençon ②   Jeanne = William, c. of Hainault ④ Ⓑ   Marguerite = Guy, c. of Blois ⑤

Carlos II = Jeanne of Navarre ②   Jeanne ⑤

Jean II

Charles V = Jeanne ①   Louis, d. of Anjou ②   Jean, d. of Berry ③   Philippe, d. of Burgundy ④

Jeanne de = Charles Ponthièvre Ⓒ

Pierre, d. = Isabelle of Bourbon ⑦

Pedro of Castile = (1) Blanche Ⓓ

217

# Acknowledgements

The photographs and illustrations in this book are reproduced by kind permission of the following. Those on pages 51, 55 and 171, by kind permission of the Controller of Her Majesty's Stationery Office; pages 18, 30, 32–3, 35, 38, 57, 61, 63, 66–67, 69, 71, 83, 88, 106, 1.16–17, 121, 136, 140, 141, 144, 150, 153, 154, 185, 190, 193, 197, 207 and 209, Trustees of the British Museum; pages 24, 26, 40, 47, 86, 130, 148–9, 151, 176–7 and 208, Bibliothèque Nationale; pages 34, 73, 74–5 and 124–5, Bodleian Library, Oxford; pages ii, 10 and 11, Judges Limited; pages 16, 76, 145 and 146, Public Record Office, London; pages 78 and 79, Society of Antiquaries of London; pages 212–13, British Tourist Authority; pages 214–15, *The Times*; page 13, Master and Fellows of Corpus Christi College, Cambridge; page 15, Royal Commission on Historical Monuments; page 58, *Crécy to Calais* by General the Honourable George Wrottlesey; page 72, Bibliothèque Royale, Brussels; page 81, The Louvre; page 84, H. Roger-Viollet; page 113, The Pierpont Morgan Library (Ms. 804, f. 128); page 152, Giraudon and St Denis; page 158, Museo Arqueologico Nacional, Madrid; page 163, Coll. Cagnières, Bibliothèque Nationale; page 166, by courtesy of the Dean and Chapter of Canterbury Cathedral; page 167, Francis Peek's *History of Stamford*; page 200, All Souls College, Oxford; and on page 204, Warburg Institute. Illustration Research Service and Celia Dearing supplied the pictures. The maps were drawn by Bucken Limited.

# Select Bibliography

*Sources*

The following are the principal contemporary sources from which the quotations in this book have been taken and, in some instances, modernized:

The Annals, Chronicles, Histories, etc., written by Avesbury, Froissart, Gray, Hemingburgh, Holinshed, Knighton, Le Baker, Le Bel, Murimuth, Stow, the Bourgeois de Valenciennes, Venette, Walsingham; the Chronicles of Lanercost, Malmesbury, Saint-Martial de Limoges, Melsa, St Albans; the *Chronique Normande du XIVe Siècle, Chronique des Quatre Premiers Valois, Grandes Chroniques de France*; Ayala's *Cronicas de los Reyes de Castilla*; Barnes's *Edward III*; Borrow's *Bible in Spain*; *The Brut*; *Calendar of Close Rolls*; Chandos Herald's *Life of the Black Prince*; Chaucer's *Parson's Tale*; Riley's *Memorials of London*; *Rolls of Parliament*; Rymer's *Foedera*; Stow's *Survey of London*; and manuscripts published in Delachenal's *Charles V*, Denifle's *Désolation des Eglises, The English Historical Review*, vol. XLI, and *Le Moyen Age*, vol. XVIII.

*Further Reading*

S. Armitage-Smith, *John of Gaunt*; A. H. Burne, *The Crécy War*; K. Fowler, *The King's Lieutenant: the First Duke of Lancaster*; H. J. Hewitt, *The Black Prince's Expedition of 1355*; J. Mackinnon, *Edward III*; M. McKisack, *The Fourteenth Century*; P. Mérimée, *Don Pedro*; P. E. L. Russell, *The English Intervention in Spain and Portugal. The University of Birmingham Historical Journal*, vol. I, has a fascinating study of Joan of Kent by M. Galway; the battles of Crécy and Poitiers and the *Grande Chevauchée* of 1355 are reconstructed at length in H. Cole's *Hawkwood*; there is an excellent bibliography for the period in *English Historical Documents, IV, 1327–1428*, ed. A. R. Myers.

# Index

222